The Liberal Case
for
Conservatism

Unemployment was a problem, so "... they said, go to, let us build us a city and a tower." Genesis 11.4 Historians offer much confusion. The Great Ziggurat of Babylon was 91 meters (300 ft) in height. Alexander the Great ordered it demolished circa 331 BCE

Log-in to health care

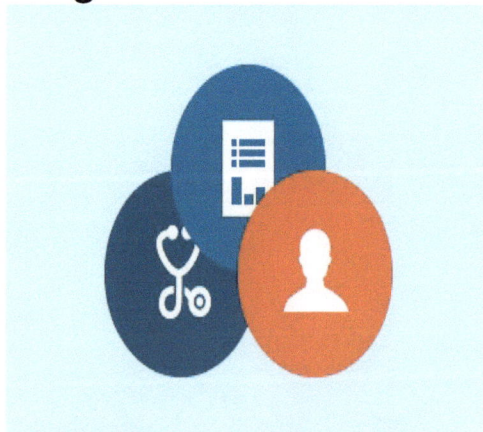

https://www.healthcare.gov

The Liberal Case

for

Conservatism

from Babel to ObamaCare

a picture book

"I am a firm believer in the people. If given the truth, they can be depended upon to meet any national crises. The great point is to bring them the real facts."

Abraham Lincoln

"The conscious and intelligent manipulation of the opinion of the masses is an important element in democratic society."

Edward Bernays

revised 1st edition Nov 2015
Addition of Ayn Rand
and the essential argument for conservatism.

Compiled by Mason A. Clark

Frontal Lobe®
Los Altos, California

Typeset in WordPerfect X3 — Images managed by Paint Shop Pro

Revised First Edition November 2015

ISBN : 978-0-931400-06-3

Printed in the United States of America

http://frontal-lobe.info

Published by Frontal Lobe®
Los Altos, California

I am an intellectual chap,
And think of things that would astonish you.

I often think it's comical
How Nature always does contrive

That every boy and every gal
That's born into the world alive
Is either a little Liberal
Or else a little Conservative!

The 1882 musing of Private Willis (not pictured)

Table of Contents

I - The History of the Dichotomy

2000 BCE – Government Jobs

Built by local free labor. With food plentiful along the Nile and a shortage of work to do, it kept the citizens employed and not revolting.

1780 BCE – Liberals Begin in Babylon

Minimum Wage in Code of Hammurabi

"If one hire a day laborer, he shall pay him from the New Year until the fifth month....six gerahs in money per day; from the sixth month to the end of the year he shall give him five gerahs per day;"

800-600 BCE – The Fifth Book of Moses: Called Deuteronomy

Rights of Labor
15:2 And this is the manner of the release: Every creditor that
lendeth ought unto his neighbour shall release it; he shall not exact
it of his neighbour, or of his brother; because it is called the
LORD's release.

24:14 Thou shalt not oppress an hired servant that is poor and needy,

Wealth Re-Distribution
24:19 When thou cuttest down thine harvest in thy field, and hast
forgot a sheaf in the field, thou shalt not go again to fetch it: it
shall be for the stranger, for the fatherless, and for the widow: that
the LORD thy God may bless thee in all the work of thine hands.

24:20 When thou beatest thine olive tree, thou shalt not go over the
boughs again: it shall be for the stranger, for the fatherless, and
for the widow.

24:21 When thou gatherest the grapes of thy vineyard, thou shalt not
glean it afterward: it shall be for the stranger, for the fatherless,
and for the widow.

Standard weights and measures
25:14 Thou shalt not have in thine house divers measures, a great and
a small.

25:15 But thou shalt have a perfect and just weight, a perfect and
just measure shalt thou have: that thy days may be lengthened in the
land which the LORD thy God giveth thee.

1215 CE – Magna Carta
THERE shall be one measure of wine throughout our kingdom, and one
measure of ale, and one measure of grain, that is the London quarter, and
one breadth of dyed cloth and of russets and of halbergets, that is two
ells within the lists; of weights, moreover, it shall be as of measures.

1723 CE – Mandeville's Fable of the Bees – Government Is the Problem

Mandeville explained:

"For the main Design of the Fable, (as it is briefly explain'd in the Moral) is to shew the Impossibility of enjoying all the most elegant Comforts of Life that are to be met with in an industrious, wealthy and powerful Nation, and at the same time be bless'd with all the Virtue and Innocence that can be wish'd for in a Golden Age."   (A long cumbersome poem; see summary in Appendix 2)

Mandeville was condemned as advocating deregulation and lawlessness.

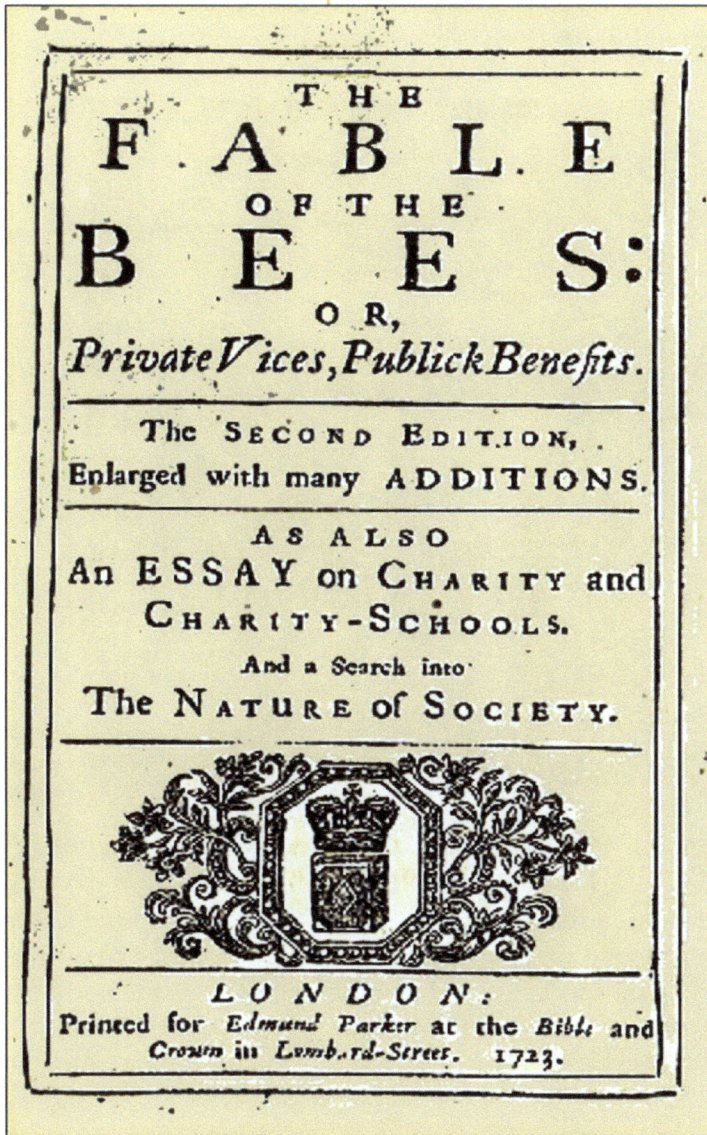

THE
F.A.B.L.E
OF THE
B E E S:
OR,
Private Vices, Publick Benefits.

The SECOND EDITION,
Enlarged with many ADDITIONS.

AS ALSO
An ESSAY on CHARITY and
CHARITY-SCHOOLS.

And a Search into
The NATURE of SOCIETY.

LONDON:
Printed for *Edmund Parker* at the *Bible* and
Crown in *Lombard-Street*. 1723.

1776 – The Declaration that Changed the World

IN CONGRESS, July 4, 1776.

The unanimous Declaration of the thirteen united States of America,

"We hold these truths to be self-evident, that all men are created equal, that they are endowed by their Creator with certain unalienable Rights,..."

"I never submitted the whole system of my opinions to the creed of any party of men whatever in religion, in philosophy, in politics, or in anything else where I was capable of thinking for myself."

"Corruption of morals in the mass of cultivators is a phaenomenon of which no age nor nation has furnished an example. It is the mark set on those, who not looking up to heaven, to their own soil and industry, as does the husbandman, for their subsistance, depend for it on the casualties and caprice of customers. Dependance begets subservience and venality, suffocates the germ of virtue, and prepares fit tools for the designs of ambition."

1776 – The Book that Changed the World: *The Wealth of Nations*

by Adam Smith:

"... and by directing that industry in such a manner as its produce may be of the greatest value, he intends only his own gain, and he is in this, as in many other cases, led by an invisible hand to promote an end which was no part of his intention."

"The interest of the dealers, however, in any particular branch of trade or manufactures, is always in some respects different from, and even opposite to, that of the public. "

"The proposal of any new law or regulation of commerce which comes from this order ought always to be listened to with great precaution,.... It comes from an order of men whose interest is never exactly the same with that of the public, who have generally an interest to deceive and even to oppress the public,...."

"…it is not very unreasonable that the rich should contribute to the public expense, not only in proportion to their revenue, but something more than in that proportion", because a tax on "the luxuries and vanities of life [which] occasion the principal expense of the rich... would in general fall heaviest upon the rich; and in this sort of inequality there would not, perhaps, be anything very unreasonable."

1788 – Edmund Burke and Tom Paine

Edmund Burke and Tom Paine had dinner together on August 18, 1788

Burke has generally been viewed as the philosophical founder of conservatism:

"Of all things, an indiscreet tampering with the trade of provisions is the most dangerous" – "To provide for us in our necessities is not in the power of government." – "The labouring people are only poor, because they are numerous." – "Wages .... bear a full proportion to the result of their labour. If we were wildly to attempt to force them beyond it, the stone which we had forced up the hill would only fall back upon them in a diminished demand."

Tom Paine was a trouble-maker in the American colonies, in France, and in England. He spent time in prison and nearly lost his head in France.

Among other of his crazy ideas (besides revolution):

A Townsend Plan: "To pay as a remission of taxes to every poor family, out of the surplus taxes,..."

Social Security: "At sixty his labour ought to be over, at least from direct necessity. It is painful to see old age working itself to death, in what are called civilised countries, for daily bread."

"... it will also be said,... that were a workman to receive an increase of wages daily he would not save it against old age,... Make, then, society the treasurer to guard it for him in a common fund; for it is no reason, that because he might not make a good use of it for himself, another should take it."

1779 – The Ancien Regime of France

Excerpt from Toqueville's "Ancien Regime..."

"Notice, I beg, how widely neighbors may be made to differ by different political principles! In the eighteenth century, in England, the only exemptions from taxes were enjoyed by the poor, in France by the rich."

"I venture to assert that when the nation ... allowed the kings to impose a tax without its consent, the nobles basely concurring on condition that they should be exempt, they sowed the seed of all the abuses and mischiefs which troubled the old regime during its existence, and led to its violent death...."

Louis XVI

1792 – Execution of Louis XVI

Marie Antoinette

1884 – Otto von Bismarck – Practical Christianity

"Practical Christianity"

Otto von Bismarck, speaking to the German Reichstag on March 20, 1884, said:

"The key point of complaint of the worker is the insecurity of his existence. He is unsure whether he will always have work; he is unsure that he will always remain healthy; and he can foresee that he will one day be old and no longer able to work. Yet if, due to lengthy illness, he falls into poverty, he is completely unable to help himself through his own efforts. Until this point in time, society has not recognized that it has any obligation to him, other than ordinary poor relief, regardless of how faithfully or industriously he previously worked. Ordinary poor relief, in addition, leaves much to be desired..."

Bismarck opened debate on the subject in November 1881 in the Imperial Message to the Reichstag, using the term *practical Christianity* to describe his program.

The Sickness Insurance Bill was passed in 1883.

Accident Insurance Law of 1884 – It paid for medical treatment and a Pension of up to 2/3s of earned wages if the worker was fully disabled.

Old Age and Disability Insurance Law of 1889 – The Old Age Pension program, an insurance equally financed by employers and workers, was designed to provide a pension annuity for workers who reached age 70 years. The Disability Insurance program was intended to be used by those permanently disabled.

Otto Eduard Leopold, Prince of Bismarck, Duke of Lauenburg

He created the first Welfare State

1910 – Teddy Roosevelt – Rough Rider, Trust Buster

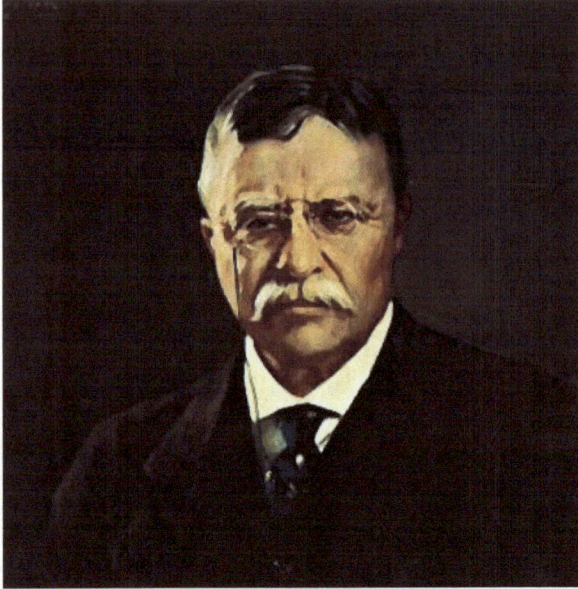

On August 31, 1910, President Theodore Roosevelt visited Osawatomie, Kansas and laid out his vision for what he called a "new nationalism."

"The object of government is the welfare of the people.'

"No man can be a good citizen unless he has a wage more than sufficient to cover the bare cost of living, "

"We need comprehensive workman's compensation acts, both State and national laws to regulate child labor and work for women, and, especially, "

"We need to enforce better sanitary conditions for our workers and to extend the use of safety appliances for workers in industry and commerce,"

"We need in our common schools not merely education in book-learning, but also practical training for daily life and work."

1933 – Franklin D. Roosevelt a later Powerful Liberal

Old Age and Disability Insurance Law: "Social Security" 1935

Socialized Medicine

"...the term 'socialized medicine' has been a powerful political weapon—even though nobody can quite define what it means. The term was popularized by a public relations firm working for the American Medical Association in 1947 to disparage President Truman's proposal for a national health care system."
T.R. Reid's 'The Healing of America'

"I believe medicare and medicaid have filled genuine needs in our society."

Ronald Reagan, Remarks at the Annual Meeting of the American Medical Association House of Delegates in Chicago, Illinois June 23, 1983

1930s – The Great Depression – the Look of Poverty

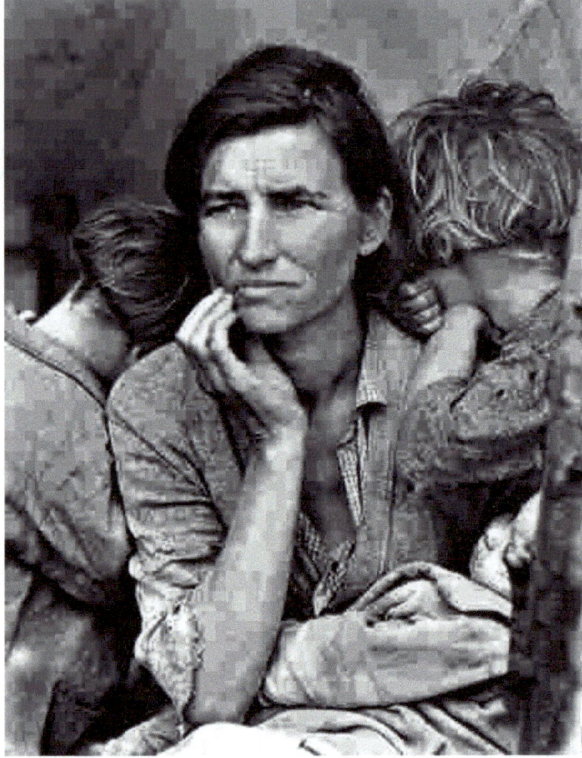

1930s – Great Depression – Men on a Bread Line

Bread Line

http://blogs.baruch.cuny.edu/his1005spring2011/tag/the-great-depression/

1933 – Communist Party Rally in New York City

More than 70,000 people at a Communist-Party rally in New York

1936 – Hooverville, Seattle, Washington

A shanty town of unemployed men.

1944 – John Maynard Keynes – Conservative

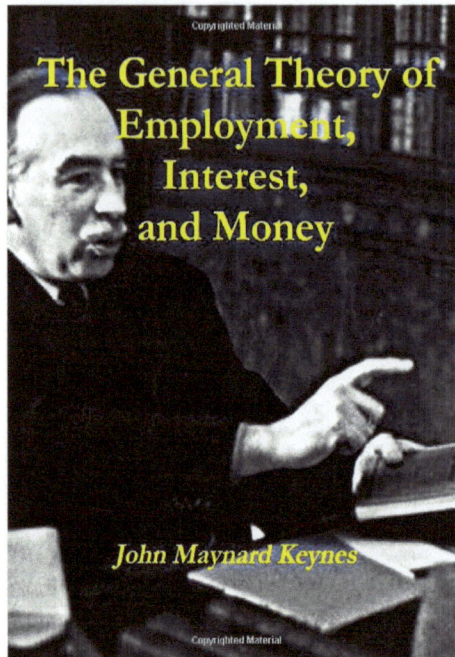

The General Theory of Employment, Interest, and Money

John Maynard Keynes

1931 – "The Problem of Unemployment"

"... now is the time for municipalities to be busy and active with all kinds of sensible improvements. "

"....why not pull down the whole of South London from Westminster to Greenwich, and make a good job of it - housing on that convenient area near to their work a much greater population than at present....,

"Would that employ men? Why, of course it would! Is it better that the men should stand idle and miserable, drawing the dole? Of course it is not.

"...the fear that we are much too poor to be able to afford what they consider to be extravagance.

Bruce Bartlett (2009): "**Keynes Was Really A Conservative.** Keynes' efforts were motivated by a strong desire to maintain the liberal capitalist order. Honest conservatives have always understood this. "

"Peter Drucker ... viewed him as not merely conservative, but *ultraconservative*. "He had two basic motivations ... One was to destroy the labor unions and the other was to maintain the free market. "Keynes was the real father of neoconservatism, far more than... Hayek! "

16

1960 – F.A. Hayek: "Why I Am Not a Conservative"

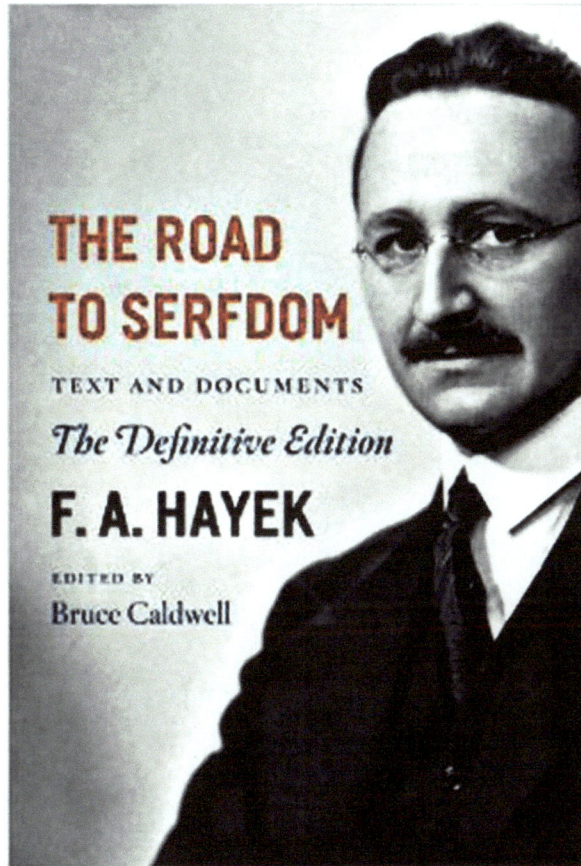

THE ROAD TO SERFDOM

TEXT AND DOCUMENTS

The Definitive Edition

F. A. HAYEK

EDITED BY
Bruce Caldwell

"Conservatism proper is a legitimate, probably necessary, and certainly widespread attitude of opposition to drastic change."

"Let me now state what seems to me the decisive objection to any conservatism which deserves to be called such. It is that by its very nature it cannot offer an alternative to the direction in which we are moving."

"...one of the fundamental traits of the conservative attitude is a fear of change.... while the liberal position is based on courage and confidence..."

"....to the liberal neither moral nor religious ideals are proper objects of coercion, while both conservatives and socialists recognize no such limits...."

"I think what is needed is a clear set of principles which enables us to distinguish between the legitimate fields of government activities and the illegitimate fields of government activity. You must cease to argue for and against government activity as such."

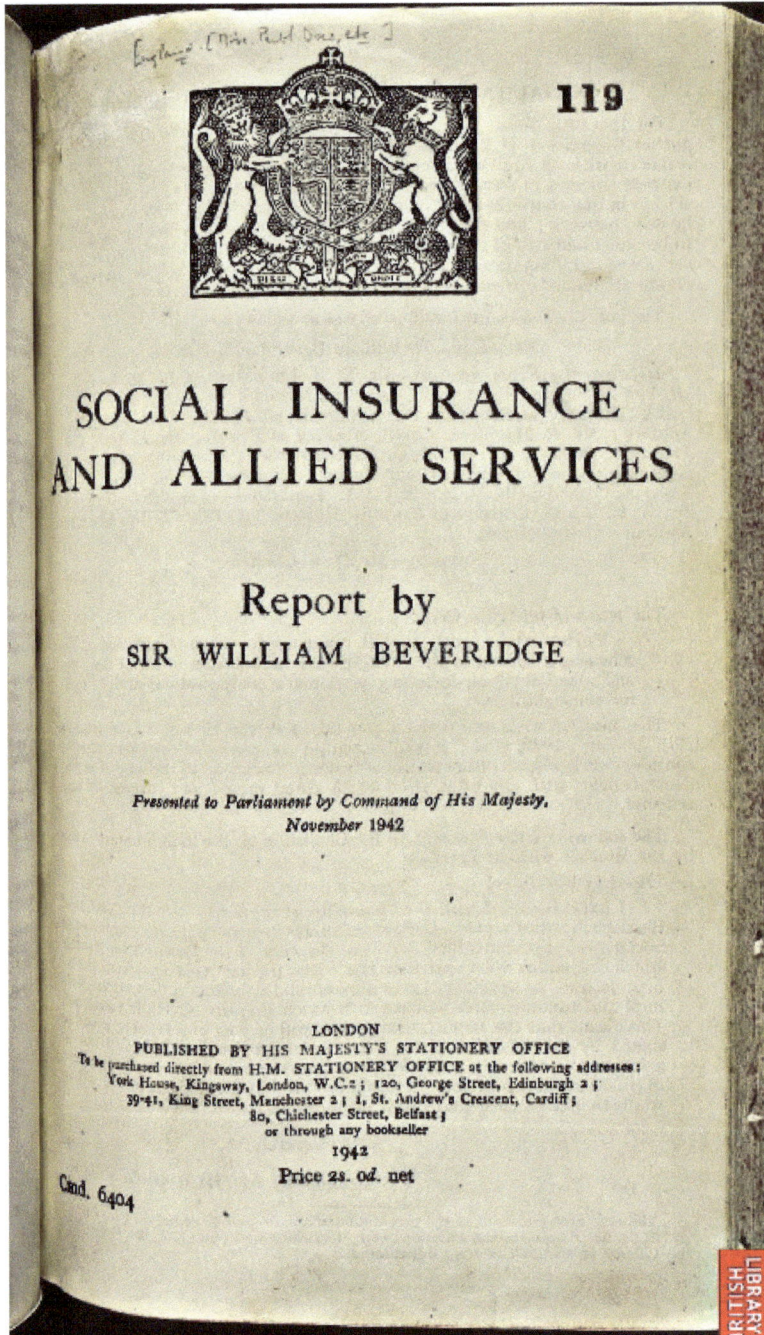

William Beveridge – British Liberal

The Beveridge Report: When the report was completed, the government seriously considered not publishing it.

The report advocated family allowances, a free health service and full employment, and that all social insurance benefits should be at flat rate and at subsistence level with the aim of abolishing poverty.

....pressure from parliament forced Prime Minister Churchill to produce plans for legislation.

The report had a major influence in other countries by setting a much more ambitious agenda for social security than had generally been accepted before.

1882 – Iolanthe – Gilbert and Sullivan – Liberals and Conservatives

Private Willis tells us:

I am an intellectual chap,
And think of things that would astonish you.

I often think it's comical
How Nature always does contrive
That every boy and every gal
That's born into the world alive
Is either a little Liberal
Or else a little Conservative!

When in that House M.P.'s divide,
If they've a brain and cerebellum, too,
They've got to leave that brain outside,
And vote just as their leaders tell 'em.

But then the prospect of a lot
Of dull M. P.'s in close proximity,
All thinking for themselves, is what
No man can face with equanimity.

Then let's rejoice with loud Fal la – Fal la la!
That Nature always does contrive

That every boy and every gal
That's born into the world alive
Is either a little Liberal
Or else a little Conservative!

1941 – From FDR to Reagan – the Four Freedoms

FDR, President Franklin Delano Roosevelt -- in his January 6, 1941 message to Congress – listed them:

1. Freedom of speech and expression.
2. Freedom to worship God in his own way
3. Freedom from want.
4. Freedom from fear.

1943 – Norman Rockwell's Four-Freedom Covers

Saturday Evening Post

http://www.setiusa.us/showthread.php?6540-Four-Freedoms-(Norman-Rockwell)

1976 – The Four Freedoms, Conservatively

In 1976 the city of Evansville, Indiana, erected a monument to the Four Freedoms but replaced freedom from want with freedom from oppression.

1. Freedom of speech and expression.
2. Freedom to worship God in his own way
3. Freedom from oppression.
4. Freedom from fear.

In Indiana, "oppression" was the code word for the regulation of business in any way.

Four Freedoms on the Home Front, Inc. had its own four freedoms:

1. Freedom from racketeering labor leaders.
2. Freedom from bureaucracy.
3. Freedom of enterprise.
4. Freedom of State and local rights.

"States Rights" had long been a code for the right to oppress African-Americans.

Ron Paul, libertarian former congressman from Texas, had a different understanding of Roosevelt's speech:

"FDR, in a well-known speech on January 6, 1941, put words to the process [of systematic attacks on the principles of liberty in his **odious Four Freedoms Speech**."

"Pursuing a policy of "freedom from want" is nothing more than a license to steal. Such a program guarantees poverty for the masses and power to the government elite."

"The idea of freedom from want and fear as a mandate of government opens up Pandora's box."

"Governments don't produce anything, so they must steal from some to give to others."

1944 – A Meaning for the Freedom from Want – FDR

An Economic Bill of Rights

An Economic Bill of Rights was proposed by President Franklin D. Roosevelt in his January 11, 1944 message to the Congress of the United States on the State of the Union:

1 – The right to a useful and remunerative job in the industries or shops or farms or mines of the nation;

2 – The right to earn enough to provide adequate food and clothing and recreation;

3 – The right of every farmer to raise and sell his products at a return which will give him and his family a decent living;

4– The right of every businessman, large and small, to trade in an atmosphere of freedom from unfair competition and domination by monopolies at home or abroad;

5 – The right of every family to a decent home;

6 – The right to adequate medical care and the opportunity to achieve and enjoy good health;

7 – The right to adequate protection from the economic fears of old age, sickness, accident, and unemployment;

8 – The right to a good education.

Note: The U.S. Supreme Court has held that:

"Though education is one of the most important services performed by the State, it is not within the limited category of rights recognized by this Court as guaranteed by the Constitution."

 SAN ANTONIO SCHOOL DISTRICT v. RODRIGUEZ, 411 U.S. 1 (1973)
411 U.S. 1

1957 - Ayn Rand

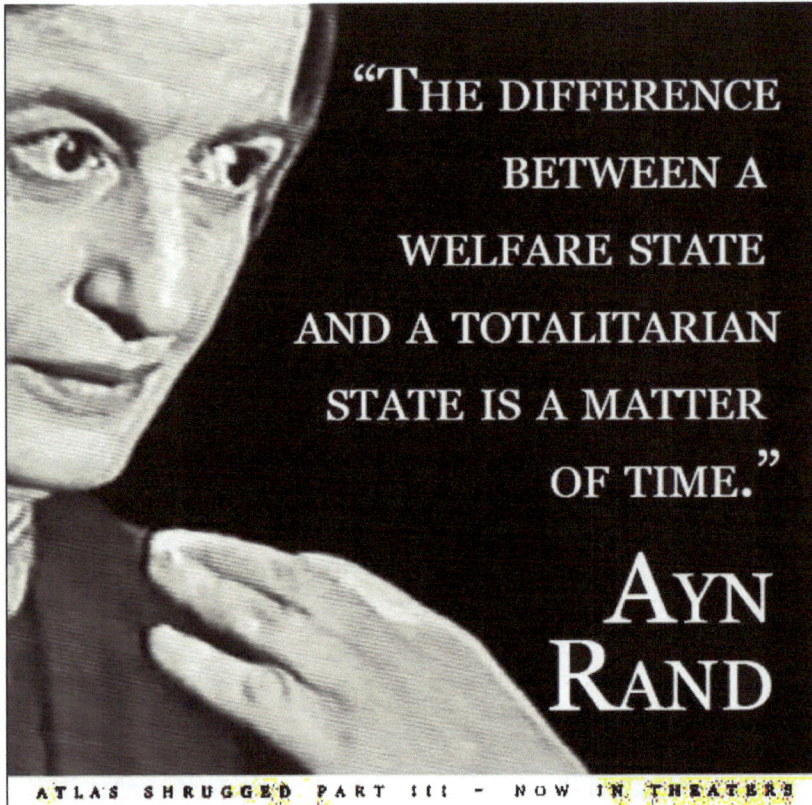

"THE DIFFERENCE BETWEEN A WELFARE STATE AND A TOTALITARIAN STATE IS A MATTER OF TIME."

AYN RAND

ATLAS SHRUGGED PART III - NOW IN THEATERS

Well known as the author of *Atlas Shrugged* and *Fountain Head*, Ayn Rand led a small "collective" with Alan Greenspan as a member. Her influence is marked by a U.S. stamp.

from Wikipedia:

"Rand advocated reason as the only means of acquiring knowledge and rejected faith and religion. She supported rational and ethical egoism, and rejected altruism. In politics, she condemned the initiation of force as immoral and opposed collectivism and statism as well as anarchism, instead supporting laissez-faire capitalism, which she defined as the system based on recognizing individual rights. .... academia generally ignored or rejected her philosophy, though academic interest has increased in recent decades....

She has been a significant influence among libertarians and American conservatives...."

24

PLAYBOY INTERVIEW of AYN RAND
 By The Editors Of Playboy from the March 1964 issue.

"I never describe my position in terms of negatives. I am an advocate of laissez-faire capitalism, of individual rights — there are no others — of individual freedom. It is on this ground that I oppose any doctrine which proposes the sacrifice of the individual to the collective, such as communism, socialism, the welfare state, fascism, Nazism and modern liberalism.

I oppose the conservatives on the same ground. The conservatives are advocates of a mixed economy and of a welfare state. Their difference from the liberals is only one of degree, not of principle."

"My views on charity are very simple. I do not consider it a major virtue and, above all, I do not consider it a moral duty. There is nothing wrong in helping other people, if and when they are worthy of the help and you can afford to help them. I regard charity as a marginal issue. What I am fighting is the idea that charity is a moral duty and a primary virtue."

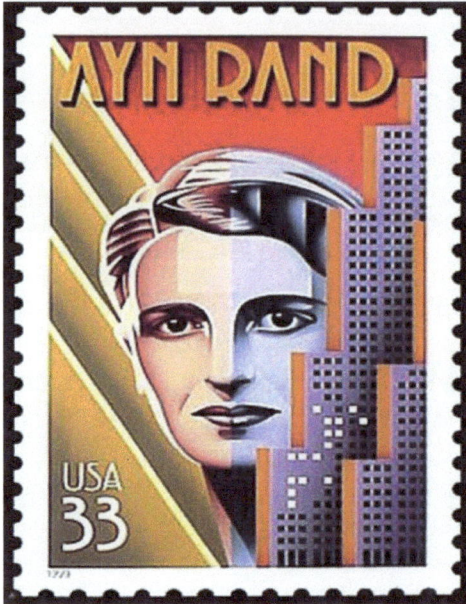

Like Franklin D Roosevelt, Ayn Rand was a stamp collector. Her stamp collection numbered to 50,000.

"Franklin D. Roosevelt (1882-1945) .... is remembered and respected for his strong yet compassionate leadership during the Great Depression and World War II....

 FDR sketched the original designs for several United States stamps issued during his time in office.

Rand's Influence on Alan Greenspan

In *The Age of Turbulence*, Alan Greenspan describes the influence that Ayn Rand had on his intellectual development.

"Ayn Rand became a stabilizing force in my life. It hadn't taken long for us to have a meeting of the minds -- mostly my mind meeting hers -- and in the fifties and early sixties I became a regular at the weekly gatherings at her apartment.

Exploring ideas with her was a remarkable course in logic and epistemology. I was able to keep up with her most of the time. Rand's Collective became my first social circle outside the university and the economics profession.

According to objectivist precepts, taxation was immoral because it allowed for government appropriation of private property by force. Yet if taxation was wrong, how could you reliably finance the essential functions of government, including the protection of individuals' rights through police power?

I still found the broader philosophy of unfettered market competition compelling, as I do to this day,

.... I'm grateful for the influence she had on my life. I was intellectually limited until I met her."

From *The Age of Turbulence* by Alan Greenspan, pp. 51-53.

1987 - Alan Greenspan, Chairman of the Federal Reserve Bank - 2006

Greenspan was Appointed by Presidents Reagan and residents George H.W.Bush and George W. Bush.

1966 – Mao Tse-Tung and his Little Red Book

"The socialist system will eventually replace the capitalist system; this is an objective law independent of man's will."

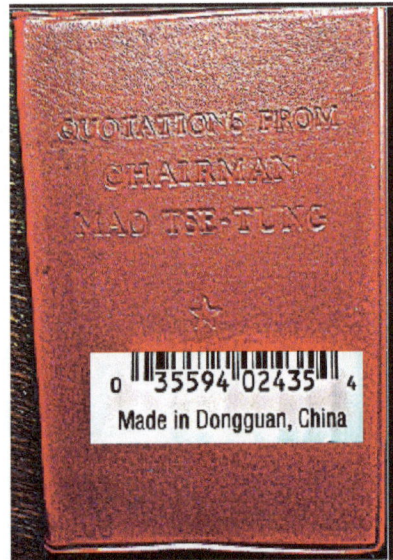

2010 – After Mao Tse-Tung – Capitalism came to China

Capitalism comes to Shanghai – a new city in twenty years.

1981 – Government is the Problem – the Leaders

Ronald Reagan:

"Government is not the solution to our problem, **government is the problem**."

"You knew that in the end it was free enterprise, not government regulation, not high taxes or big government spending, but free enterprise, that had led to the building of a great America."

"If we continue to combat needless regulations, we can keep the economy from suffocating beneath red tape. If we prevent government from mandating additional costs on business."

Margaret Thatcher's restatement of Mandeville's "Fable of the Bees" thought:

"Adam Smith's 'invisible hand' is not above sudden, disturbing, movements. ....'gales of creative destruction' still roar mightily from time to time. To lament these things is ultimately to **lament the bracing blast of freedom itself**." —

Ronald Reagan: in Berlin June 12, 1987: "**Mr. Gorbachev, tear down this wall.**"

(The wall came down November 9, 1989)

30

1961-1989 – The Berlin Wall – Soon to Fall

1991 – The Fall of Stalin and the End of the USSR

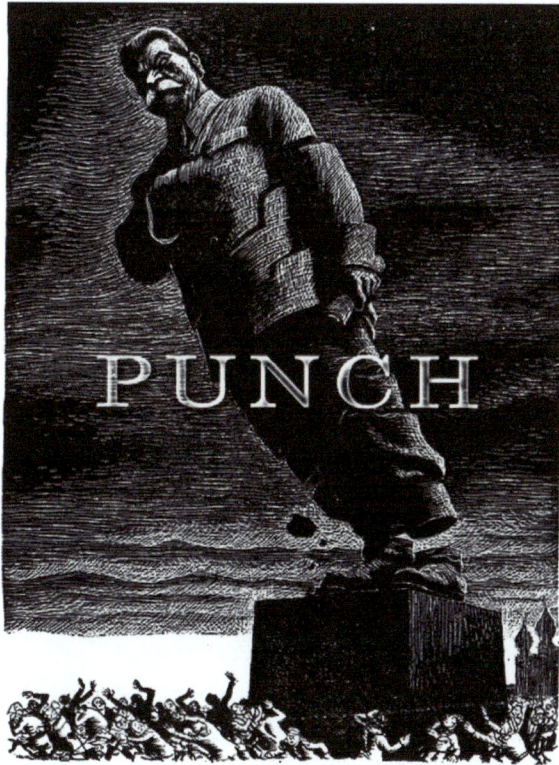

1991 – The Losses of the USSR Empire

EASTERN BLOC MEMBERS
- Satellite States
- USSR-aligned until 1948
- USSR-aligned until 1960

SOVIET UNION

POLAND

EAST GERMANY

CZECHOSLOVAKIA

HUNGARY

ROMANIA

YUGOSLAVIA

BULGARIA

ALBANIA

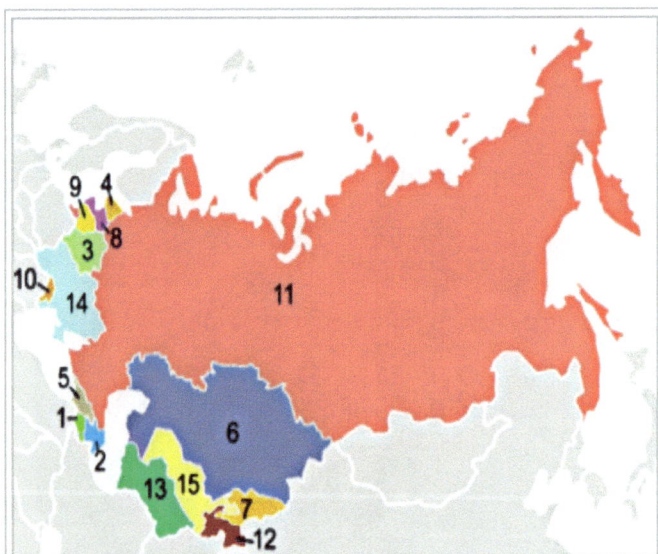

Post-Soviet states in English alphabetical order:
1. Armenia; 2. Azerbaijan; 3. Belarus; 4. Estonia;
5. Georgia; 6. Kazakhstan; 7. Kyrgyzstan; 8. Latvia;
9. Lithuania; 10. Moldova; 11. Russia; 12. Tajikistan;
13. Turkmenistan; 14. Ukraine; 15. Uzbekistan

1991 – "The Stairway to Lenin" – the ending

"The Orchestra .... finishes with the rising rhythm of Ravel's Bolero, on a flight of stairs that represents the long march of communism, until its inevitable and definitive collapse."

'Stairway to Lenin...' from "The Orchestra"
Conceived & directed by Zbig Rybczynski
Music: 'Bolero' by Maurice Ravel (1875-1937)
Orchestra RIAS Berlin/Ferenc Fricsay
"The Orchestra" (Zbig Vision, Ltd.)
'Films and Videos by Zbig Rybczynski'
www.zbigvision.com / chrisw@filmsbyzbig.com

2010 – The Supreme Court – The Final Say

CONSERVATIVE: Chief Justice John Roberts Samuel Alito Clarence Thomas, Antonin Scalia

UNCERTAIN CONSERVATIVE Anthony Kennedy

LIBERAL: Stephen Breyer, Ruth Bader Ginsburg Elena Kagan, Sonia Sotomayor

In a 2010 case known as "Citizens United," the majority wrote, "If the First Amendment has any force, it prohibits Congress from fining or jailing citizens, or associations of citizens, for simply engaging in political speech."

"Associations of citizens" includes corporations, making corporations citizens for this purpose. Do corporations have a right to vote? That is not yet decided.

The "speech" in question was money. That money is speech with free speech rights was advocated in by Buckley v. Valeo, 424 U.S. 1 (1976)

"A restriction on the amount of money a person or group can spend on political communication during a campaign necessarily reduces the quantity of expression by restricting the number of issues discussed, the depth of their exploration, and the size of the audience reached."

A century earlier:

On August 31, 1910, President Theodore Roosevelt visited Osawatomie, Kansas and laid out his vision for what he called a "new nationalism."

"The Constitution guarantees protection to property, and we must make that promise good. But it does not give the right of suffrage to any corporation."

"There can be no effective control of corporations while their political activity remains. To put an end to it will be neither a short nor an easy task, but it can be done."

"It is necessary that laws should be passed to prohibit the use of corporate funds directly or indirectly for political purposes"

"Necessary" but not carved in stone, as is Teddy.

"Citizens United was "the most misguided, naive, uninformed, egregious decision of the United States Supreme Court I think in the 21st century."
~~Senator John McCain

1970, 1987 – Greed is Good?

The businessmen believe that they are defending free enterprise when they declaim that business is not concerned "merely" with profit but also with promoting desirable "social" ends....

"Businessmen who talk this way are unwitting puppets of the intellectual forces that have been undermining the basis of a free society these past decades."

but:

"...Quaker Oats president Kenneth Mason, writing in Business Week, declared Friedman's profits-are-everything philosophy "a dreary and demeaning view of the role of business and business leaders in our society… Making a profit is no more the purpose of a corporation than getting enough to eat is the purpose of life. Getting enough to eat is a requirement of life; life's purpose, one would hope, is somewhat broader and more challenging. Likewise with business and profit."

"Greed is good."

Gordon Gekko of "Wall Street" fame

2010 – Tea Party Rally in Washington, D.C.

In an ad for the National Review, 2014:

> We battle fortnightly using grace, wit, and élan to expose the liberal boneheads, bozos, cranks, dupes, dweebs, head cases, philistines, pinkos, and whiners who are muddying public discourse with their bleating about the parlous state of our democracy.
>
> Something must be done.

William Buckley, founder of the National Review

Abe Lincoln may have freed all men but Sam Colt made them equal.

II - The Welfare State

Welfare, public housing projects – UK and US

First Public Housing

In the United Kingdom in 2010, 17% of households were in social housing – in part an effect of housing destruction in World War II.

A Medieval Almshouse in England – one solution to poverty

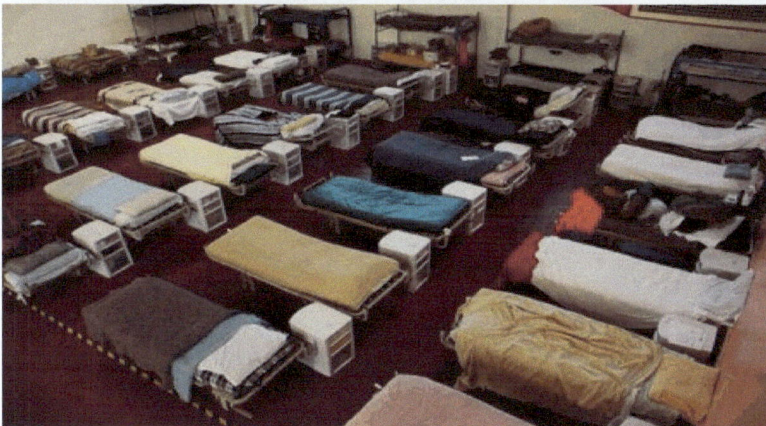

Housing for Homeless, United States, 2014

Housing: Mother Cabrini, Chicago, built 1942-1962

Built 1942-1962. Demolished 2011.

http://upload.wikimedia.org/wikipedia/commons/0/0a/Cabrini_green.jpg

Pruitt-igoe Housing Project in St. Louis, Missouri

Built 1955-1956. Demolished 1972-1975

More Food Stamps, Less Welfare, More Food-Stamp Welfare

Fewer Receiving Welfare, But Food Stamps Soaring

The number of Americans receiving cash welfare has fallen since the 1990s, while the number receiving food stamps has risen sharply.

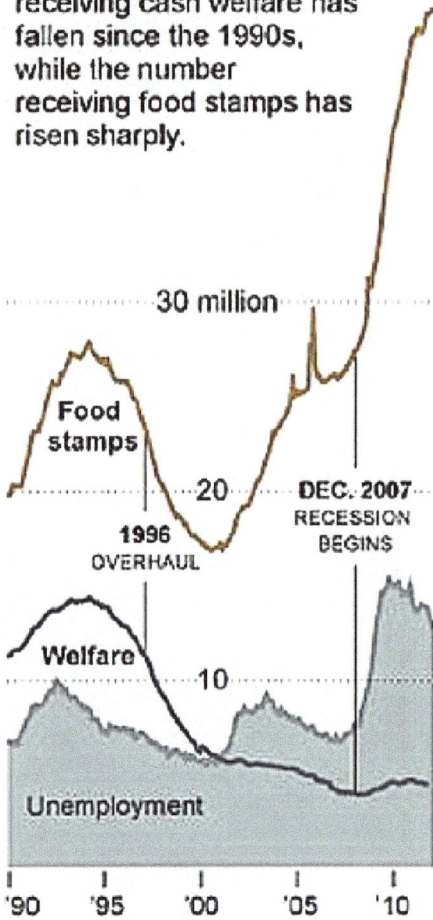

30 million

Food stamps

20

DEC. 2007
RECESSION
BEGINS

1996
OVERHAUL

Welfare

10

Unemployment

'90   '95   '00   '05   '10

Sources: U.S. Dept. of Health and Human Services (welfare); U.S. Dept. of Agriculture (food stamps); Bureau of Labor Statistics

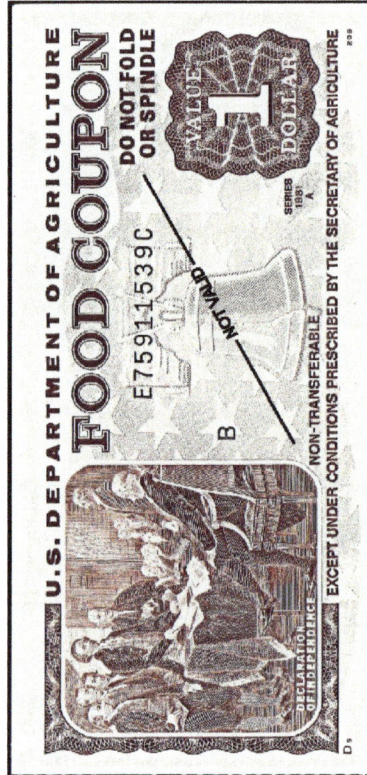

U.S. DEPARTMENT OF AGRICULTURE

FOOD COUPON

DO NOT FOLD OR SPINDLE

VALUE 1 DOLLAR

SERIES 198 A

E7591.1539C

NON-TRANSFERABLE

EXCEPT UNDER CONDITIONS PRESCRIBED BY THE SECRETARY OF AGRICULTURE

B

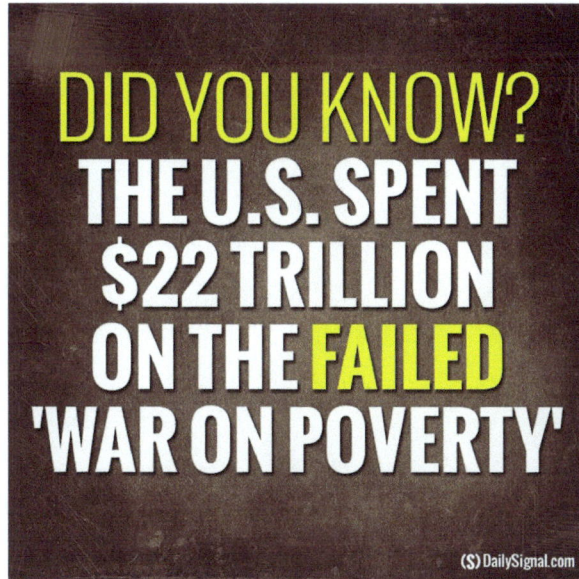

See "Ignore the Missing Facts" at end of this book

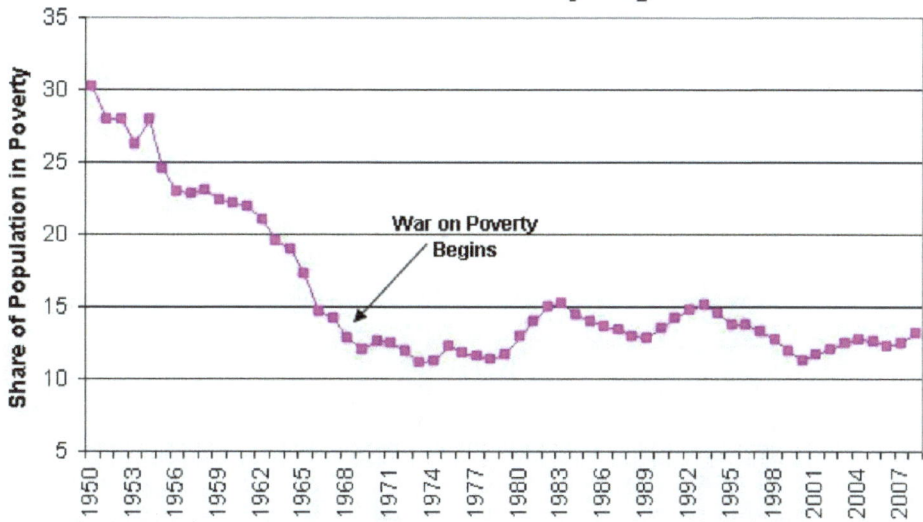

See "Ignore the Missing Facts" at end of this book

A Wealth of Food Most of Us Can Afford

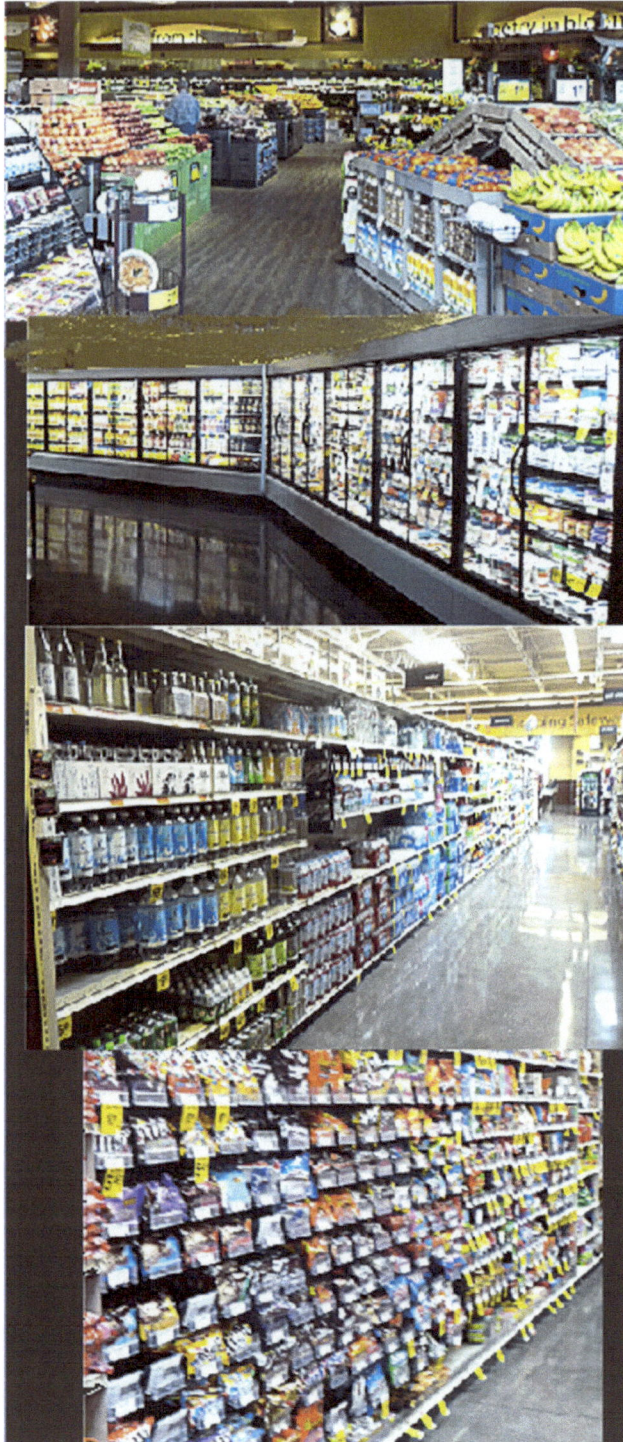

Safeway, California

III - Inequality – The Fruits of the Earth

"The first man who, having fenced in a piece of land, said 'This is mine,' and found people naïve enough to believe him, that man was the true founder of civil society.... Beware of listening to this impostor; you are undone if you once forget that the fruits of the earth belong to us all, and the earth itself to nobody."

Jean-Jacques Rousseau, 'Discourse on Inequality' – 1754

"When all the objectives of government include the achievement of equality -- other than equality before the law – that government poses a threat to liberty."

Margaret Thatcher, Statecraft: Strategies for a Changing World – 2002

Just to remind us – who started the welfare state? A tough guy:

The Wealth Distribution in the United States

1 % of the population has 33.4 % of the net worth
4 % has 25.8 %
5 % has 12.3 %
10 % has 12.9 %
 20 % has 11.3 %
 20 % has 3.9 %
 40 % has 0.3 %

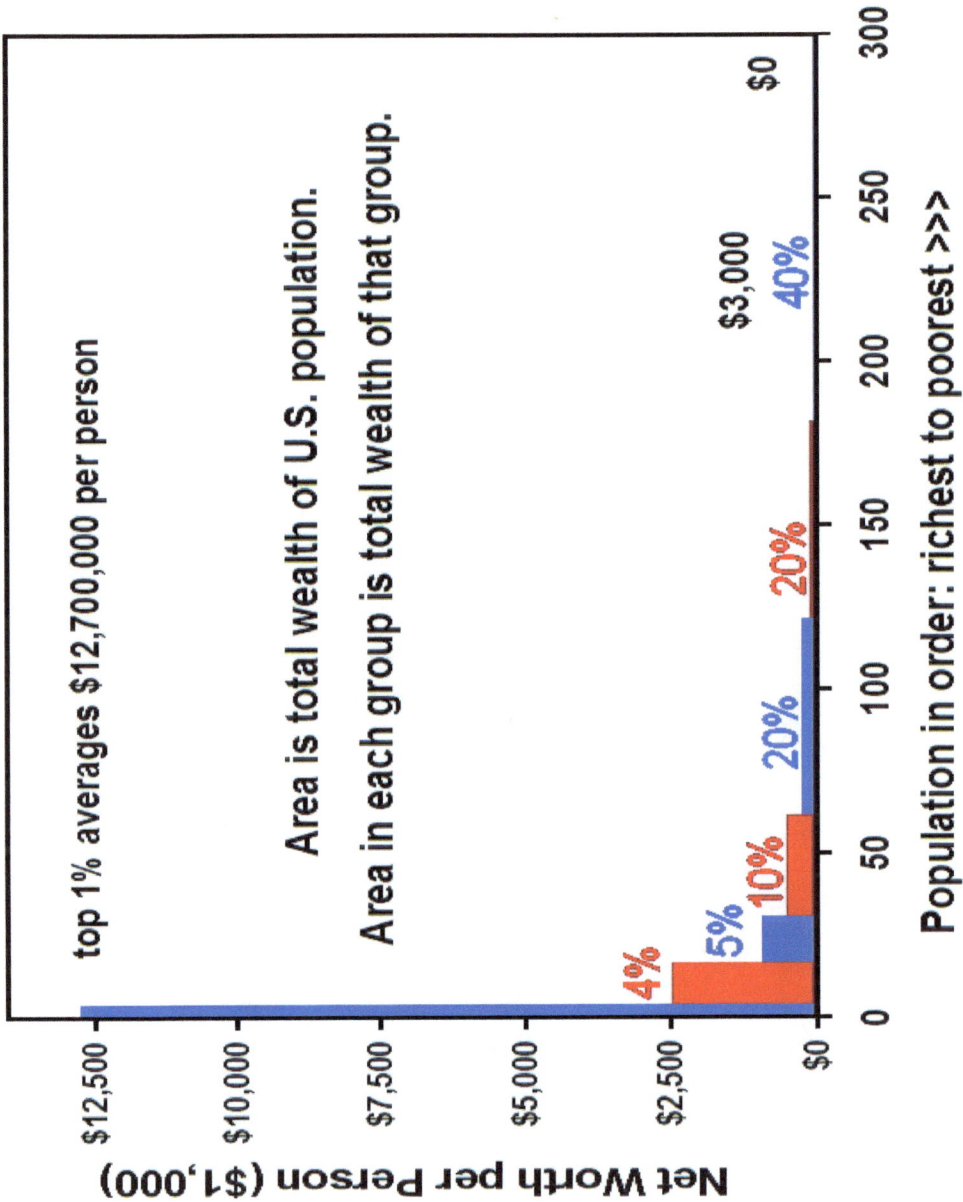

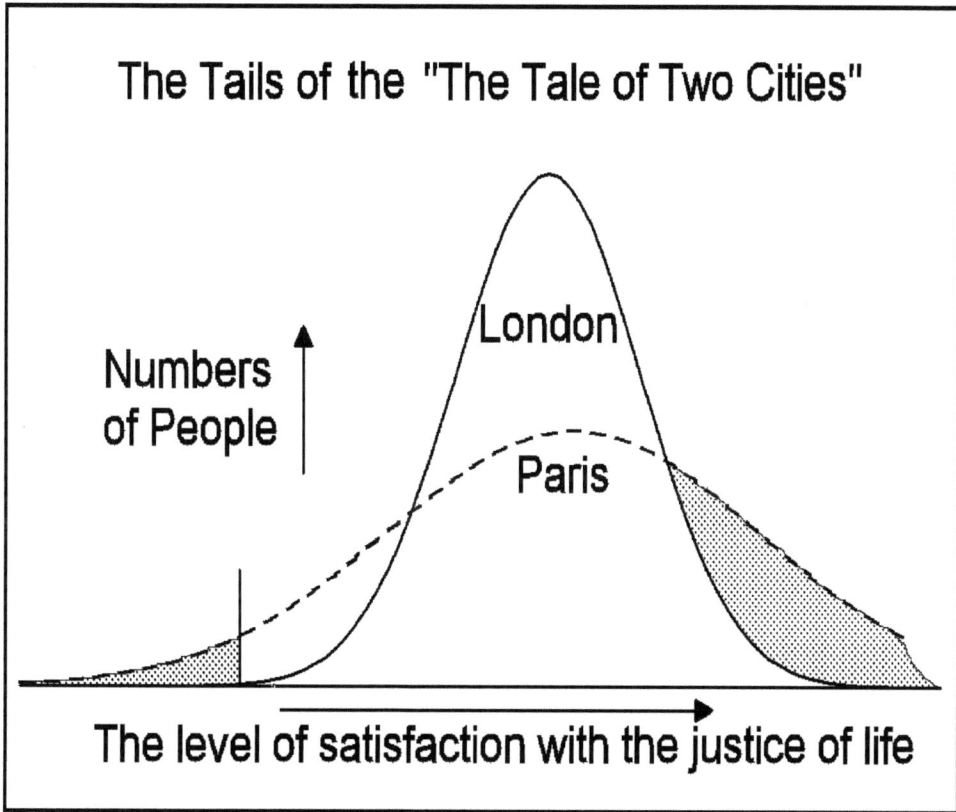

The Tails of the "The Tale of Two Cities"

Numbers of People

London

Paris

The level of satisfaction with the justice of life

In the tail on the left lived the French Revolution and the guillotine..
Some 40,000 members of the tail on the right were beheaded.

Poverty – the left tail – leads to revolt, commonly violent.

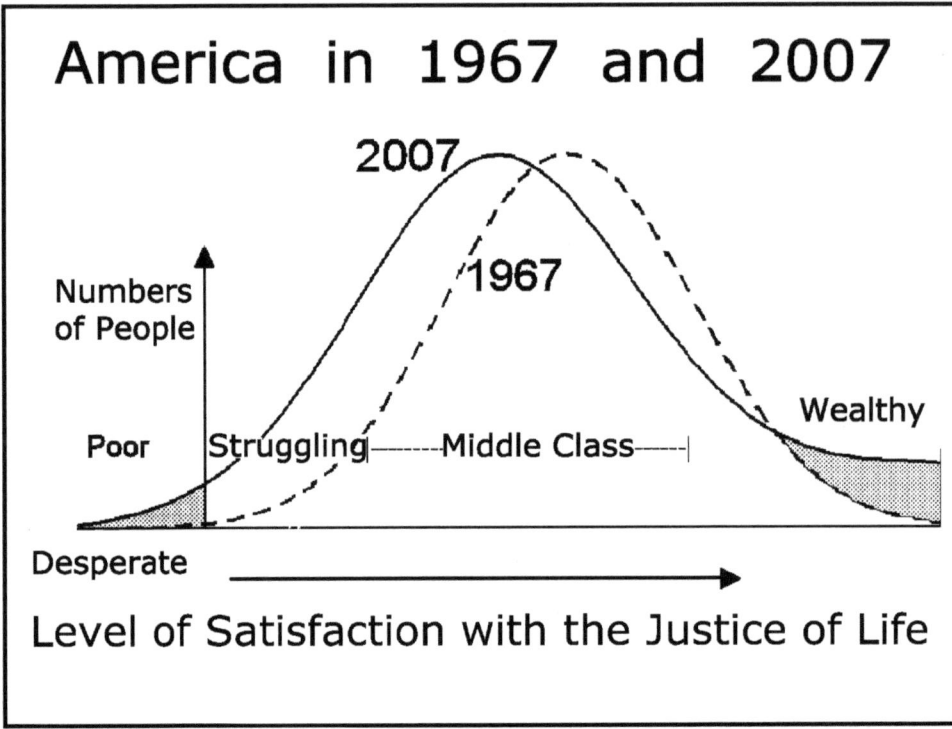

America in 1967 and 2007

In wealthy America, few Americans are poor – certainly by comparison with Paris of 1790 or most of the world of 2014. But if one subtracts all "welfare" of the welfare state, Americans are reported to live in poverty.

Poverty – the left tail – leads to robberies, among other problems

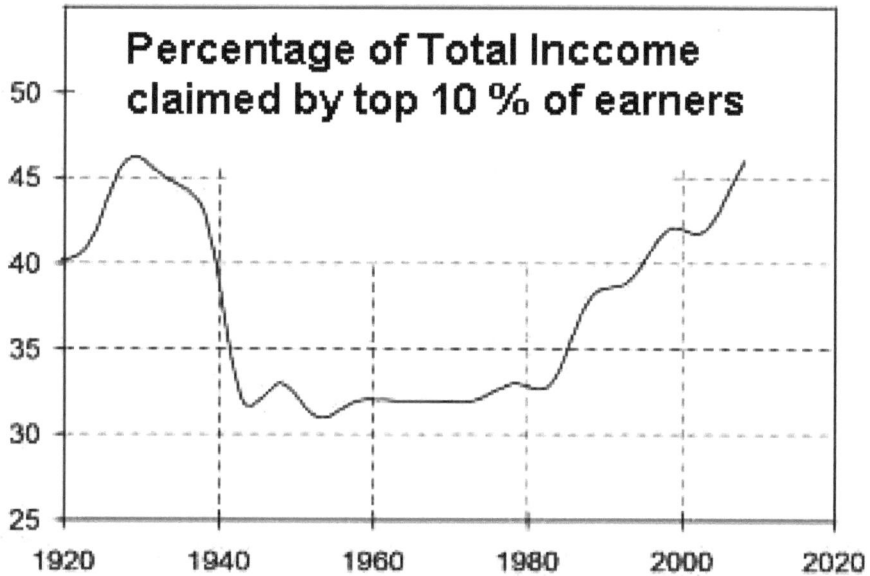

Percentage of Total Inccome claimed by top 10 % of earners

The years from 1946 to 1970 are called the "Golden Era" – the years when the "Greatest Generation" prospered.

Income Distribution – 1920 to 2020

Buffett stated that he only paid 19% of his income for 2006 ($48.1 million) in total federal taxes ... while his employees paid 33% of theirs .. He bragged:

"There's class warfare, all right, but it's my class, the rich class, that's making war, and we're winning."

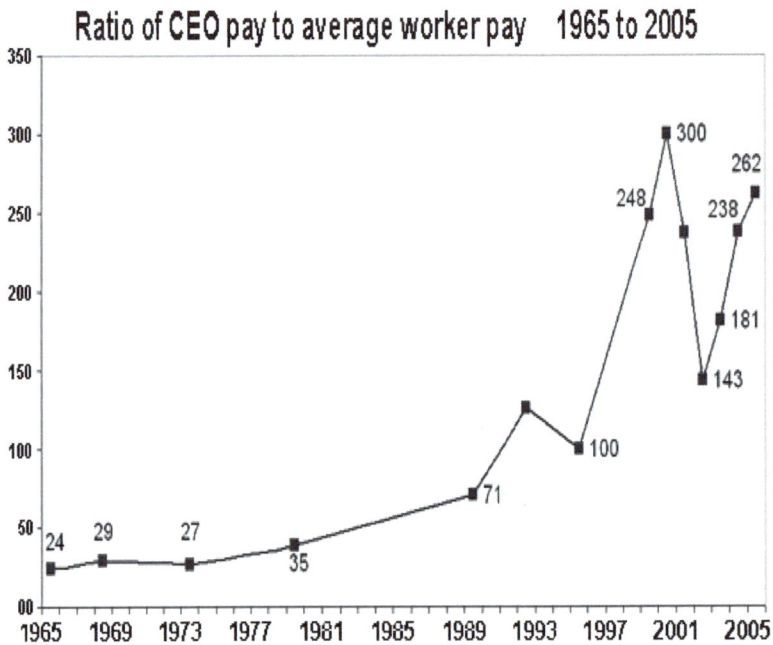

Source: Mishel, Bernstein, and Allegretto, The State of Working America 2006/07

Are the Rich Winning the Class War?

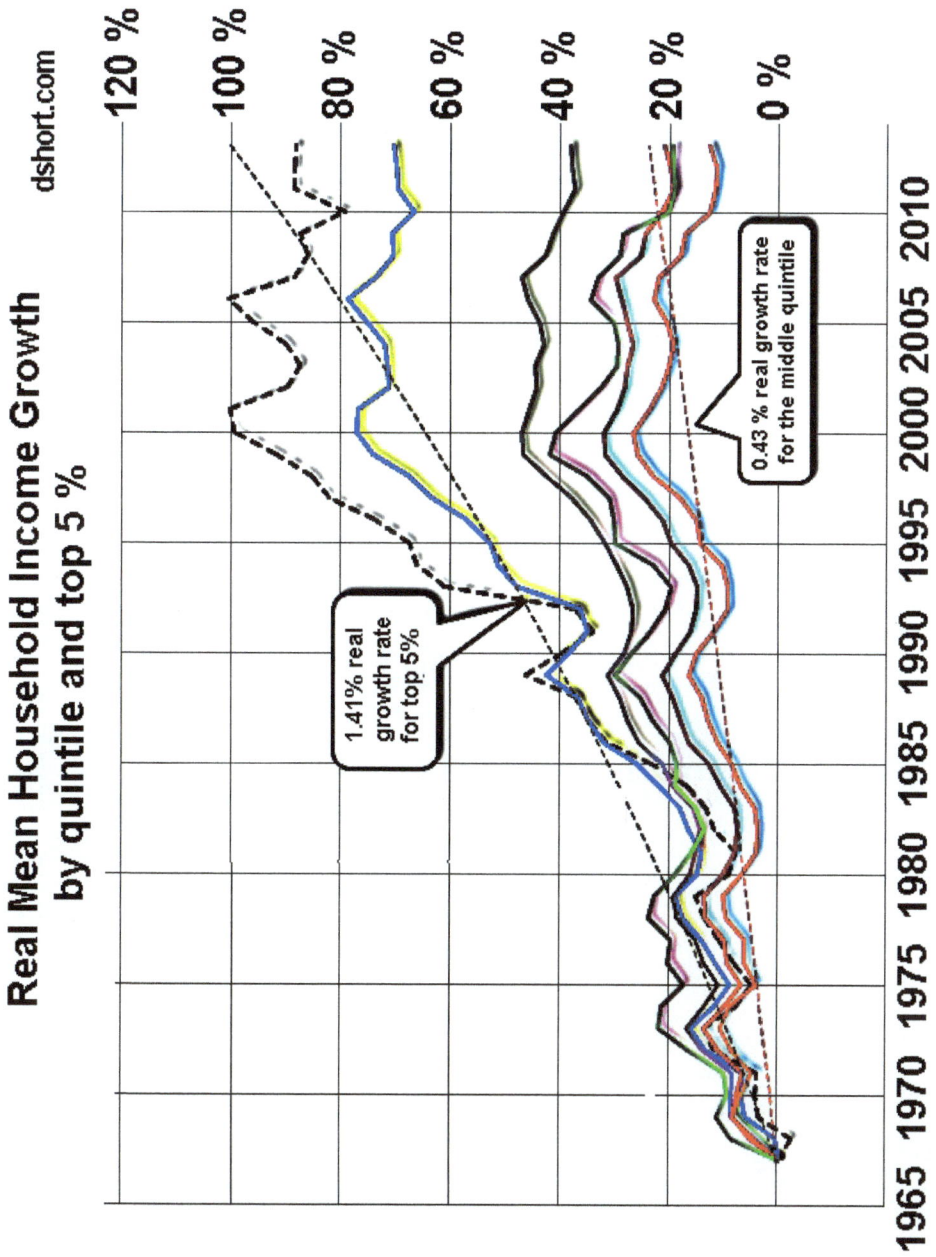

Real Mean Household Income Growth by quintile and top 5 %

dshort.com

1.41% real growth rate for top 5%

0.43 % real growth rate for the middle quintile

Adam Smith and Henry Ford

Adam Smith in his 1776 classic, The Wealth of Nations:

"It is but equity... that they who feed, clothe and lodge the whole body of the people, should have such a share of the produce of their own labor as to be themselves tolerably well fed, clothed and lodged."

And:

"The necessity of civil government grows up with the acquisition of valuable property" and "Till there be property there can be no government, the very end of which is to secure wealth, and to defend the rich from the poor."

Henry Ford thought the worker should be able to buy his Model T.

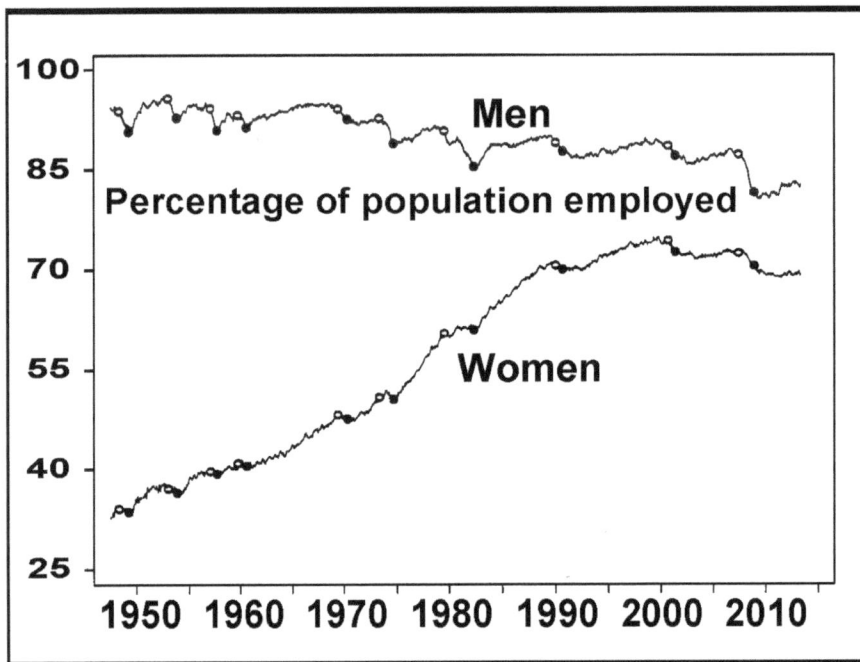

To have enough – or to have more – women have gone to work. Henry Ford needs a working women to help the working men buy there Ford's. The consequences are too numerous and too serious to find a place here.

Poverty in America

The nation's official poverty rate in 2013 was 14.5 percent, down from 15.0 percent in 2012. The 45.3 million people living at or below the poverty line in 2013, for the third consecutive year, did not represent a statistically significant change from the previous year's estimate.

News Release September 16, 2014 by U.S. Census Bureau

But, compiled from U.S. government sources by the Heritage Foundation:

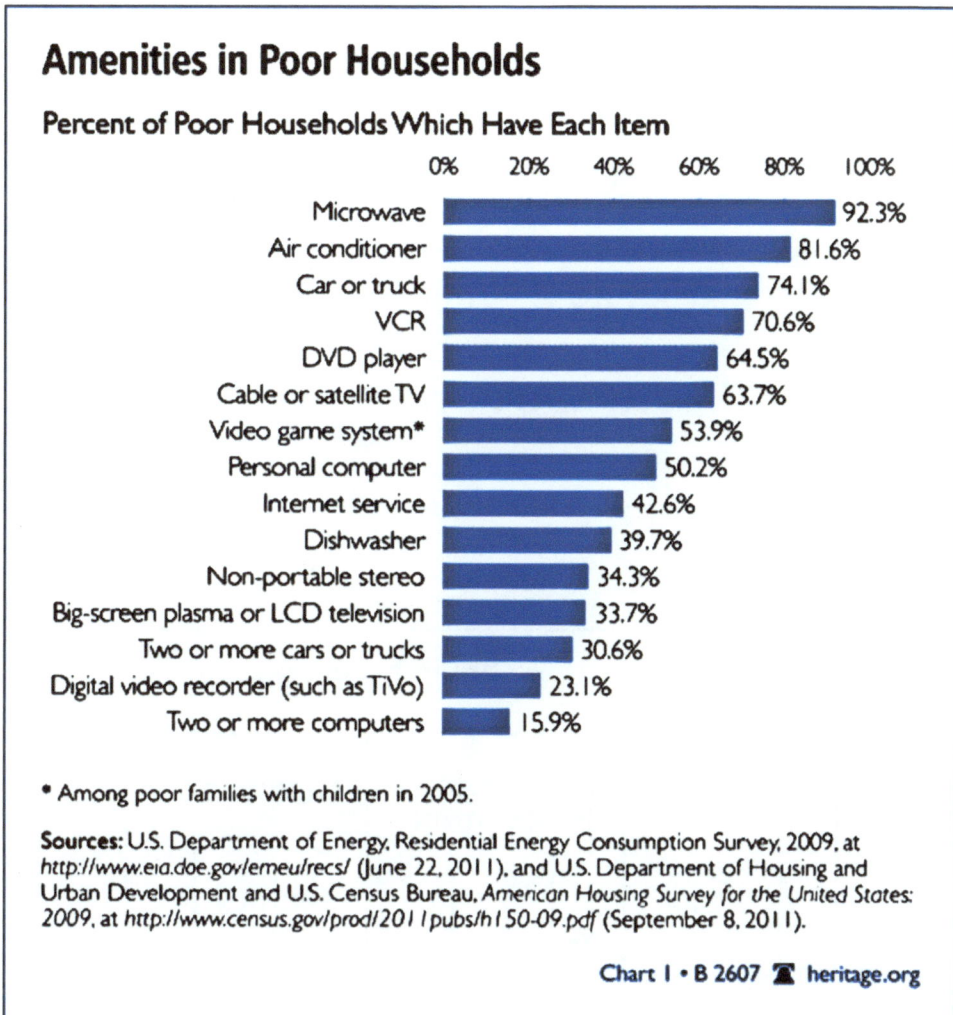

Amenities in Poor Households

Percent of Poor Households Which Have Each Item

Item	Percent
Microwave	92.3%
Air conditioner	81.6%
Car or truck	74.1%
VCR	70.6%
DVD player	64.5%
Cable or satellite TV	63.7%
Video game system*	53.9%
Personal computer	50.2%
Internet service	42.6%
Dishwasher	39.7%
Non-portable stereo	34.3%
Big-screen plasma or LCD television	33.7%
Two or more cars or trucks	30.6%
Digital video recorder (such as TiVo)	23.1%
Two or more computers	15.9%

* Among poor families with children in 2005.

Sources: U.S. Department of Energy, Residential Energy Consumption Survey, 2009, at http://www.eia.doe.gov/emeu/recs/ (June 22, 2011), and U.S. Department of Housing and Urban Development and U.S. Census Bureau, *American Housing Survey for the United States: 2009,* at http://www.census.gov/prod/2011pubs/h150-09.pdf (September 8, 2011).

Chart 1 • B 2607 ☎ heritage.org

IV - The Role of Government

The Myths of Government Accounting

Confusion of Expenses, Investments, Distributions

Picture 1 -- the Popular Myth

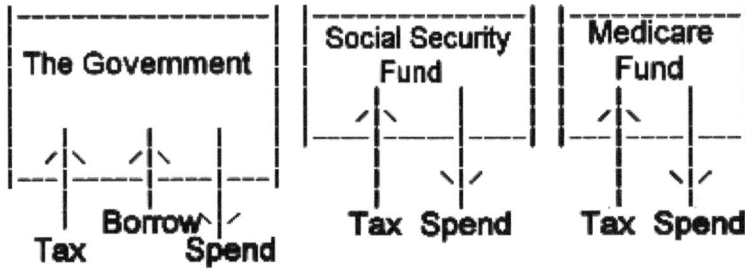

The Government	Social Security Fund	Medicare Fund
Tax Borrow Spend	Tax Spend	Tax Spend

Picture 2 -- the Reality

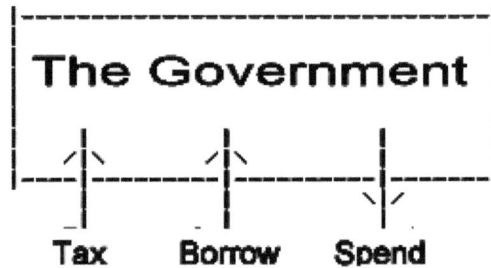

The Government

Tax   Borrow   Spend

Picture 3   As it should be accounted

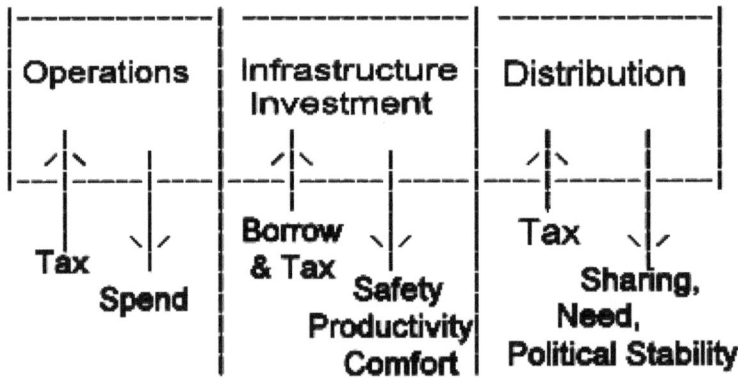

Operations	Infrastructure Investment	Distribution
Tax Spend	Borrow & Tax Safety Productivity Comfort	Tax Sharing, Need, Political Stability

The Federal Government is Shrinking

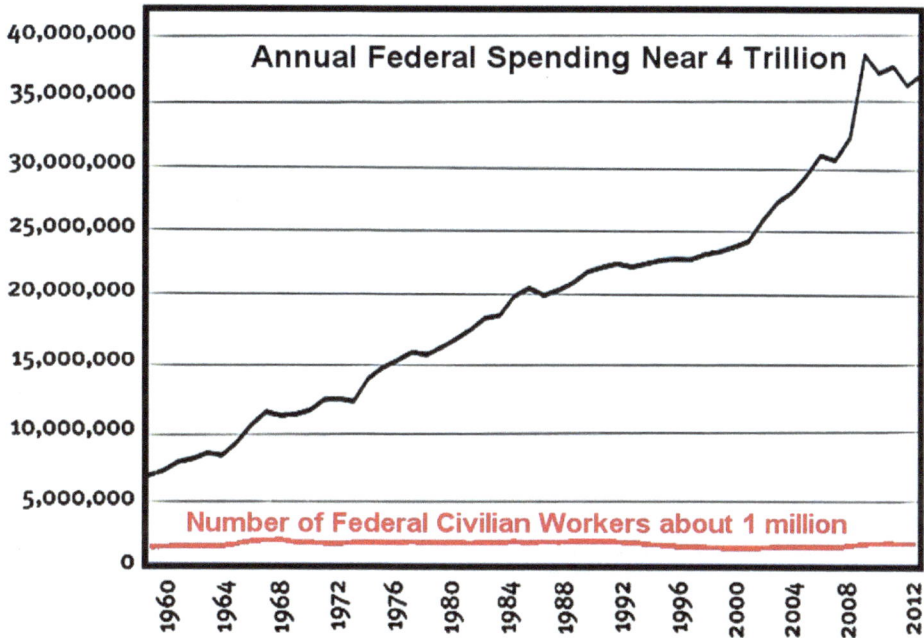

Annual Federal Spending Near 4 Trillion

Number of Federal Civilian Workers about 1 million

Edited from the cover of the book: **Bring Back the Bureaucrats** by John J. DiIulio, reviewed favorably in the conservative National Review October 2014

DiIulio suggests: "Revitalize good government by hiring (one million) people to do all the jobs Americans want government to do.

The increased Federal Spending counts distribution as spending. It is not.

"Distribution" is not "spending." It buys nothing. Spending is for purchases, including employees wages, and grants. Real spending has been static for decades while more actions have been demanded.

The Shrinking Government

The Federal government has been getting smaller. But transfers have been growing, impelled by income and wealth inequality and by special interests.

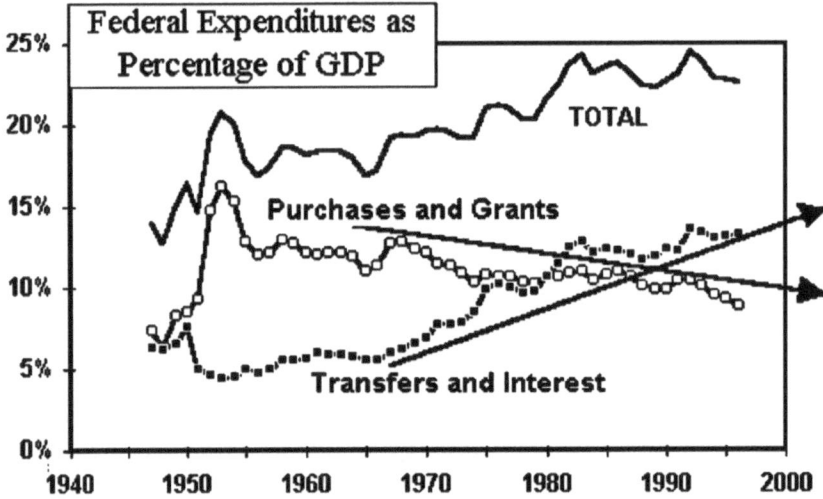

Federal Government about 2014 about $3.8 trillion

Transfers including Interest about $2.65 trillion

Health	$ 1,045 B	Medicare is here
Pensions	$ 969 B	Social Security is here
Welfare	$ 386 B	
Interest	$ 252 B	

Purchases "spent" about $1.15 trillion

Defense	$ 840 B
Education	$ 131 B
Transportation	$ 98 B
Government	$ 48 B
Protection	$ 34 B

Please feel free to insert your own numbers – enjoy.

The Question of the Debt

"Because of the debt, we cannot afford health care."

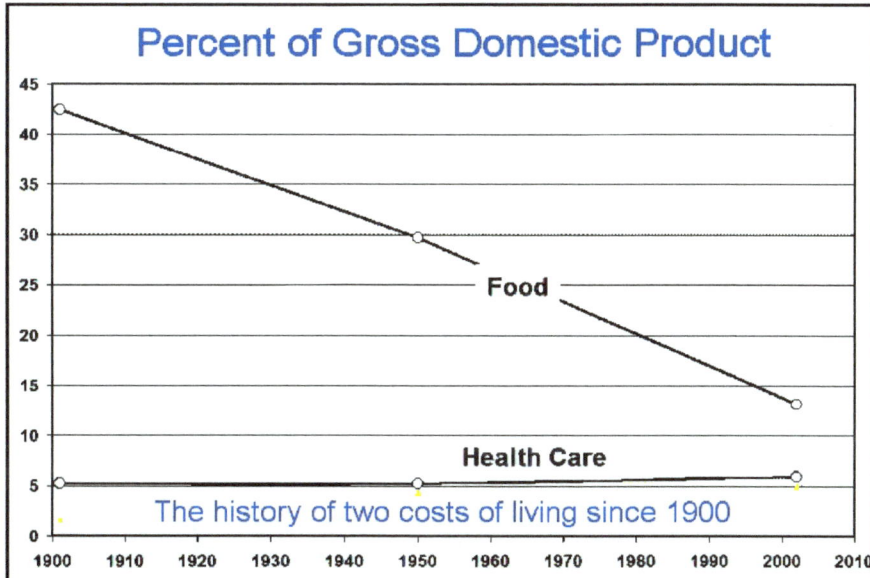

Percent of Gross Domestic Product

Food

Health Care

The history of two costs of living since 1900

Health Care – Affordable?

In 2014 we are "not able to afford universal health care" at 8 percent of the GDP.

In 1950 we were not able to eat with the cost being 30 percent of the GDP.

Is it a Liberal-Conservative question?

Social Security

"Social Security today has a $2.6 trillion dollar surplus, can pay out every benefit owed to every eligible American for the next 27 years and has not contributed one nickel to the deficit. This is an ideological struggle on the part of Republicans in Congress and their billionaire backers to undo the most significant government social program in the history of the United States."

Senator Bernie Sanders 2014

See also: Sanders' comment elsewhere on infrastructure spending.

Sanders was reelected in 2012 with 71% of the vote. He has said he is "prepared to run for President of the United States" in 2016

(comment. Social Security has no surplus stored in a strong-box. Sander's "surplus" is an accounting fiction not of his making.)

A Day in the Life – One Man's Experience

Joe gets up and prepares his morning coffee. He fills his pot full of good clean drinking water meeting government minimum water quality standards.

He takes his daily medication with his first swallow of coffee. His medications are safe to take because laws insure they are safe and work as advertised.

All but $10.00 of his medications are paid for by his employers medical plan because some union workers fought their employers for paid medical insurance.

He prepares his morning breakfast with bacon and eggs. Joe's bacon is safe to eat because laws regulate the meat packing industry since the time of Upton Sinclair's 1906 novel, The Jungle .

Joe takes his morning shower reaching for his shampoo; His bottle is properly labeled with every ingredient and the amount of its contents because of regulations guaranteeing his right to know what he was putting on his body.

Joe dresses, walks outside and takes a deep breath. The air he breathes is clean because of laws to stop industries and automobiles from polluting our air.

He walks to the subway station for his government subsidized ride to work.

Joe has a good job with excellent pay, medicals benefits, retirement, paid holidays and vacation because union members fought and died for these working standards. Joe's employer pays these standards because Joe's employer doesn't want his employees to call the union.

If Joe is hurt on the job or becomes unemployed he'll get a worker compensation or unemployment check from the government.

At noon time, Joe makes a Bank Deposit so he can pay some bills. Joe's deposit is federally insured by the FDIC.

Joe drives to visit his father at his farm home in the country. His car is among the safest in the world because of laws and regulations for car safety standards.

His father's didn't have electricity until big government provided rural electrification.

He is happy to see his dad who is now retired and lives on Social Security and his union pension.

Joe tells his father. "We don't need big government ruining our lives; after all, I'm a self made man who believes everyone should take care of themselves, just like I have."

Edited from:

A Day in the Life of Joe Middle-Class Republican
by John Gray, Cincinnati, Ohio, July 2004 (copyright implicit)
Published by permission but edited without permission.

A Day in the Life – Executives Blunder

LETTERS TO THE EDITOR, San Jose Mercury News, March 1993

Executives for Clinton have blundered   I am very disappointed that John Young, John Sculley and many of my other good friends in the Silicon Valley industry have been caught in the updraft of Bill Clinton's hot air balloon.

I share their concern about the platform of the Republican Party and the influence of right-wing deviates centered in Orange County.

My friends have overlooked the fact that the Democratic Party has been the party of socialism since President Roosevelt's term in the Great Depression of the 1930's. I was there, and I recall vividly the NRA (National Recovery Administration), which was referred to as 'nuts, raspberries and applesauce.

The great contribution of free enterprise including scientists and engineers under the leadership of Vannevar Bush during World War II made America the strongest nation in the world.

Roosevelt's disastrous agreement with Stalin at Yalta was a clear signal that he fundamentally supported socialism rather than freedom.

Gov. Clinton's military experience is limited to calling up the National Guard in one of our smaller, less important states.

If Pat Schroeder, Barbara Boxer and many other leading Democrats had had their way during the past 20 years, the United States, under President Bush's leadership, could not have undertaken Desert Storm, which was the greatest military victory in the history of the world.

The Democratic Party is indentured to union labor and has expressed opposition to the North American Free trade Agreement, which will generate millions of jobs in Canada, the United States and Mexico in the years ahead.

The Democratic Party is also indentured to the teachers' union. As long as the teachers' union places survival ahead of the need to have knowledge about the subject being taught, there is no hope of improving American's educational system.

These and other similar evaluations of well- established Democratic Party positions convince me that my friends, who have defected to support Clinton, are making a serious strategic mistake.

David Packard Chairman of the Board, Hewlett-Packard Co.

A List of Government Things from FDR to Obama

Glass-Steagal act limiting bank gambling, repealed; banks collapsed in 2008
Interstate Highway System; (F.D.Roosevelt proposed this system but it was the
 conservative, Eisenhower, who carried it out.)
GI Bill (had strong conservative support)
Labor Laws
Marshall Plan
Environmental Laws
Food safety laws
Workplace safety laws
Social Security
Space Program
Peace corps
Civil Rights act signed by Lyndon Johnson (the South switches to Republican
The Internet
The Tennessee Valley project
Women's right to vote
Universal Public Education (land grants)
National Weather Service
Scientific Research
Product Labeling; Truth in Advertising Laws
Public Health
Morrill Land Grant Act
Rural Electrification
Public Universities
Bank Deposit Insurance
Earned Income Tax Credit
Centers for Disease Control and Prevention
Family and Medical Leave Act
Consumer Product Safety Commission
Public Broadcasting
Americans With Disabilities Act
Clean Air Act 1963
and....

The Prime Argument for Conservatism – difficult to make

It was the purpose of this book to present the essental reason, the raison d'être, for conservatism. This proved too difficult. I could find no way to do this. The book was a failure, but an elegant failure.

Let me try a bit here:

People need, just have, a motivation. Historically, the hunter-gatherer motivation was the prospect of starvation. Everyone worked. Everyone had a job. There was no such thing as unemployment. Charity, compassion for the unable, was a development that waited increased efficiency in hunting, in gathering, and in growing: the invention of agriculture. With a surplus came that charity along with the pleasure of waging war and building empires, small then large.

When charity became governmental function called the "welfare state," there came loss of motivation to a part or all of the population. The welfare state expanded in some nations to the "managed state" of which invention of the centrally-governed economies, commonly called "communist."

A notable example was East Germany from 1949 to 1990. In Wikipeida we read:

"No worker could be sacked, unless for serious misconduct or incompetence; even in such cases, alternative work would be offered. The GDR had no system of unemployment benefit because the concept of unemployment did not exist.

With a very low birth rate and a high rate of exodus, East Germany was losing workers. As the goal of socialism is the elimination of capitalist economics, the GDR strove to reduce wealth disparity between individuals through the elimination of private property, businesses and stores. While enforcement of this ideal led to a more economically even society, it prompted many with economic ambition or those who did not agree with its enforcement to escape—typically those with higher education: doctors, scientists, engineers, and skilled workers. This growing loss of skilled personnel was intended to be curtailed with the building of the wall

An East German.psychiatrist asserted on a TV interview that it take a generation for the East German workers to adapt to the rigors of life in a "free society" where workers could be fired for low production (or, one might add, for working under the influence of vodka).

But I have not been able to document this and even to suggest it draws charges of racism, nationalism, prejudice, and other sins. Hence the failure of this book.

Perhaps a reader will help me. My e-mail address can be found on my website.

IV - Public Works
Remedies for Unemployment:

Pyramids, Cathedrals, War

North Korean military parade, 4/15/2012 (AP)

Hoover Dam – Employment in the Great Depression

Mandeville (he of the Bee Fable) in his "An Essay on Charity..." points out public works that could employ the poor – an alternative to charity.:

"There is above three or four Hundred Years Work, for a Hundred Thousand Poor more than we have in this Island. To make every part of it Useful, and the whole thoroughly inhabited, many Rivers are to be made Navigable, Canals to be cut in Hundreds of Places. Some Lands are to be drain'd and secured from Inundations for the future: Abundance of barren Soil is to be made fertile, and thousands of Acres rendered more beneficial by being made more accessible."

Done with Imported Labor   2003 to 2010

the tallest man-made structure in the world, at 2,722 feet

Burj Khalifa, Dubai

Here, government has built a mosque (a "cathedral") inside a government city, the "Defense Housing Authority" within the city of Karachi, Pakistan.

Masjid e Tooba, built in 1969 in Defence Housing Authority, Karachi, Pakistan
The DHA is an 8,852 acre government city within a city

Public Works Administration – PWA

Triborough Bridge - PWA project
http://docs.fdrlibrary.marist.edu/photo.cgi

The PWA epitomized the Rooseveltian notion of "priming the pump" to encourage economic growth. The PWA funded the construction of more than 34,000 projects, including airports, electricity-generating dams, and aircraft carriers; and seventy percent of the new schools and one third of the hospitals built during that time.

Works Progress Administration – WPA

"W.P.A.", a 1939 song recorded by Louis Armstrong and The Mills Brothers: "Sleep while you work while you work rest while you play / Lean on your shovel to pass the time away".

    (a personal note: my father's pride kept him from the WPA at a time when he desperately needed work – he hated the sight of men leaning on shovels.)

but, wikipedia tells us:

"The Work Projects Administration... employ[ed] millions of unemployed people (mostly unskilled men) to carry out public works projects, including the construction of public buildings and roads. The WPA employed musicians, artists, writers, actors and directors in large arts, drama, media, and literacy projects."

"Almost every community in the United States had a new park, bridge or school constructed by the agency.... Between 1935 and 1943, the WPA provided almost eight million jobs."

"Robert Leighninger asserts that ".... the Public Works Administration, the Works Progress Administration, and the Civilian Conservation Corps built facilities in practically every community in the country. Most are still providing service half a century later. It is time we recognized this legacy and attempted to comprehend its relationship to our contemporary situation."

Rural Electrification Administration – REA

In 1930, only 13 percent of farms had electricity.

Farm life dramatically improved with power for lights, refrigeration, appliances, and farm equipment. Electricity powered labor-saving machines. Electric water pumps powered many irrigation pumps on the farm and cisterns for running water in kitchens and indoor bathrooms.

Space Shuttle – Jobs Jobs Jobs – $196 Billion

"The companies involved in space applications are all over the country, from rocket motor manufacturers like Rocketdyne and Aerojet in California, to fastener manufacturers on the East Coast," says Plucker. "I would be hard pressed to think of a state without an impact.

Federally Funded Research and Development Centers

Aerospace Federally Funded Research and Development Center
Ames Laboratory
Argonne National Laboratory
Arroyo Center
Brookhaven National Laboratory
Center for Advanced Aviation System Development
Center for Communications and Computing
Center for Enterprise Modernization
Center for Naval Analyses
Center for Nuclear Waste Regulatory Analyses
Centers for Medicare and Medicaid Services Federally Funded Research and Development Center
Fermi National Accelerator Laboratory
Frederick National Laboratory for Cancer Research
Homeland Security Studies and Analysis Institute
Homeland Security Systems Engineering and Development Institute
Idaho National Laboratory
Jet Propulsion Laboratory
Judiciary Engineering and Modernization Center
Lawrence Berkeley National Laboratory
Lawrence Livermore National Laboratory
Lincoln Laboratory
Los Alamos National Laboratory
National Biodefense Analysis and Countermeasures Center
National Center for Atmospheric Research
National Defense Research Institute
National Optical Astronomy Observatory
National Radio Astronomy Observatory
National Renewable Energy Laboratory
National Security Engineering Center
Oak Ridge National Laboratory
Pacific Northwest National Laboratory
Princeton Plasma Physics Laboratory
Project Airforce
Sandia National Laboratories
Savannah River National Laboratory
Science and Technology Policy Institute
SLAC National Accelerator Laboratory
Software Engineering Institute
Systems and Analyses Center
Thomas Jefferson National Accelerator Facility

Los Alamos National Laboratory, New Mexico

Idaho National Laboratory

The Pure Food and Drug Act - now FDA

Pure Food and Drug Act

Long title	An act for prefenting the manufacture, sale or transportation of adulterated or misbranded or poisonous or deleterious foods, drugs medicines, and liquors, and for regulating traffic therein, and for other purposes.
Acronyms (colloquial)	PFDA
Enacted by	the 59th United States Congress
Effective	June 30, 1906

Legislative history

- Introduced in the Senate as S. 88 by Weldon Heyburn (R–ID) on December 14, 1905
- Passed the Senate on February 21, 1906 (63-4 🔊)
- Passed the House on June 20, 1906 (143-72 🔊)

Amount Per Serving

Calories 100   Calories from Fat 0

	% Daily Value*
Total Fat 0g	**0%**
Saturated Fat 0g	**0%**
Trans Fat 0g	
Polyunsaturated Fat 0g	
Monounsaturated Fat 0g	
Cholesterol 0mg	**0%**
Sodium 125mg	**5%**
Potassium 90mg	**3%**
Total Carbohydrate 23g	**8%**
Dietary Fiber 2g	**8%**
Sugars 13g	
Protein 1g	

Vitamin A 0%   •   Vitamin C 0%

Calcium 4%   •   Iron 4%

*Percent Daily Values are based on a 2,000 calorie diet. Your daily values may be higher or lower depending on your calorie needs:

	Calories:	2,000	2,500
Total Fat	Less than	65g	80g
Sat Fat	Less than	20g	25g
Cholesterol	Less than	300mg	300mg
Sodium	Less than	2,400mg	2,400mg
Potassium		3,500mg	3,500mg
Total Carbohydrate		300g	375g
Dietary Fiber		25g	30g

INGREDIENTS: FIGS, WHOLE GRAIN WHEAT FLOUR, SUCROSE, UNBLEACHED ENRICHED FLOUR (WHEAT FLOUR, NIACIN, REDUCED IRON, THIAMINE MONONITRATE (VITAMIN B1), RIBOFLAVIN (VITAMIN B2), FOLIC ACID), HIGH FRUCTOSE CORN SYRUP, CORN SYRUP, GLYCERIN, WHEY (FROM MILK), SALT, SOY LECITHIN*, LEAVENING (BAKING SODA, CALCIUM PHOSPHATE), CALCIUM LACTATE, SODIUM BENZOATE AND SULFUR DIOXIDE (SULFITES) ADDED TO PRESERVE FRESHNESS, MALIC ACID, NATURAL AND ARTIFICIAL FLAVOR.

*ADDS A TRIVIAL AMOUNT OF FAT.

CONTAINS: WHEAT, MILK, SOY.

MONDELEZ GLOBAL LLC
EAST HANOVER, NJ 07936 USA
MADE IN MEXICO

V - Infrastructure

San Bruno, Calif. Gas-line Fire

Power Grid

www.nature.com/news/us-electrical-grid-on-the-edge-of-failure

Transportation

Cars from a Metro-North Railroad passenger train are scattered after the train derailed in the Bronx neighborhood of New York... http://www.poughkeepsiejournal.com/ Dec 7, 2013

"How come we are not investing heavily in rebuilding our country's infrastructure? One trillion dollars invested in building roads, bridges, water systems (will provide) 13 million decent paying jobs."

Senator Bernie Sanders 2014

There was talk of his running for President.

(In 2012 Sanders was reelected Senator for Vermont with 71% of the vote.)

74

Our Aging Capital Stock
(average age of structures, equipment, and software)

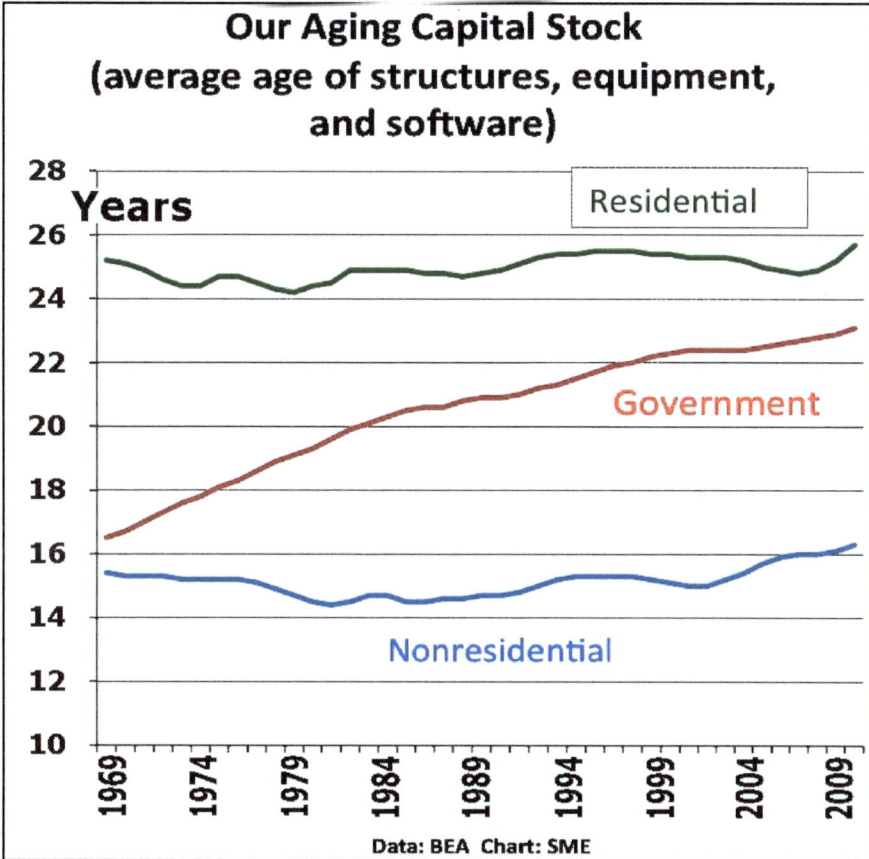

Years

Residential

Government

Nonresidential

28
26
24
22
20
18
16
14
12
10

1969 1974 1979 1984 1989 1994 1999 2004 2009

Data: BEA Chart: SME

AMERICA'S GPA:

D⁺

ESTIMATED INVESTMENT NEEDED BY 2020:

$3.6 TRILLION

The American Society of Civil Engineers is committed to protecting the health, safety, and welfare of the public, and as such, is equally committed to improving the nation's public infrastructure. To achieve that goal, the Report Card depicts the condition and performance of the nation's infrastructure in the familiar form of a school report card—assigning letter grades that are based on physical condition and needed investments for improvement.

Transportation Safety

General Motors Finances Ralph Nader
Liberal versus Conservative

On March 22, 1966, GM President James Roche was forced to appear before a United States Senate subcommittee, and to apologize to Nader for the company's campaign of harassment and intimidation.

Nader later successfully sued GM for excessive invasion of privacy. The money from this case allowed him to lobby for consumer rights.

Former GM executive John DeLorean asserted that Nader's criticisms were valid. Former Ford and Chrysler President Lee Iacocca said the Corvair was 'unsafe' and a 'terrible' car.

United States $ 640 $B
China $ 188 B
Russia $ 88 B
Saudi Arabia $ 67 B
France $ 61 B
U.K. $ 58 B
Germany $ 49 B
Japan $ 49 B
India $47 B

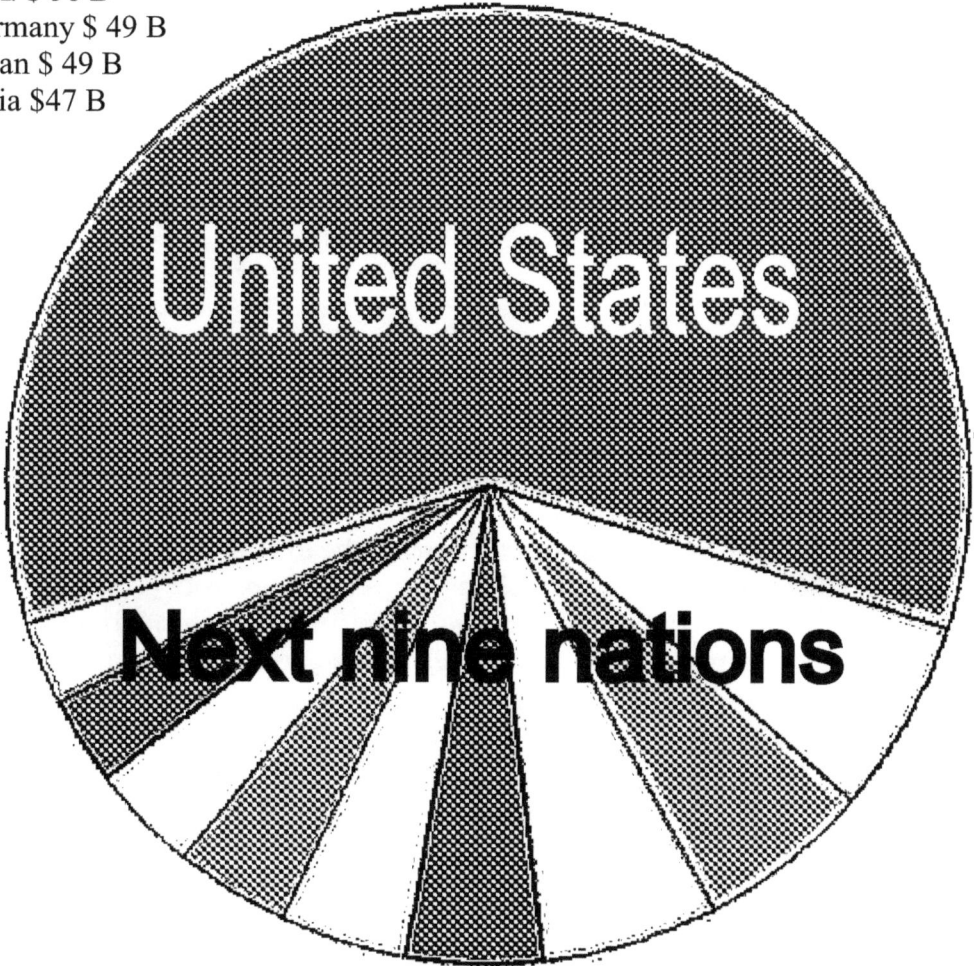

A President and Former General Spoke

"Every gun that is made, every warship launched, every rocket fired signifies, in the final sense, a theft from those who are hungry and are not fed, those who are cold and are not clothed. The world in arms is not spending money alone. It is spending the sweat of its laborers, the genius of its scientists, the hopes of its children..."

President Dwight Eisenhower, 1953

in his Farewell Address:

"This conjunction of an immense military establishment and a large arms industry is new in the American experience. The total influence-economic, political, even spiritual, is felt in every city, every state house, every office of the Federal government. We recognize the imperative need for this development. Yet we must not fail to comprehend its grave implications....

"In the councils of government, we must guard against the acquisition of unwarranted influence, whether sought or unsought, by the military-industrial complex. The potential for the disastrous rise of misplaced power exists and will persist."

"Our people expect their President and the Congress to find essential agreement on issues of great moment, the wise resolution of which will better shape the future of the Nation"

"In this final relationship, the Congress and the Administration have, on most vital issues, cooperated well, to serve the national good rather than mere partisanship, and so have assured that the business of the Nation should go forward. So, my official relationship with the Congress ends in a feeling, on my part, of gratitude that we have been able to do so much together."

American Military Sites

American Military Sites		
Afghanistan	Greece	Netherland Antil.
American Samoa	Greenland	Oman
Antigua	Guam	Pakistan
Aruba	Honduras	Peru
Australia	Hong Kong	Portugal
Austria	Iceland	Puerto Rico
Bahamas	Diego Garcia	Qatar
Bahrain	Indonesia	Saudi Arabia
Belgium	Italy	Singapore
Bosnia	Japan	Spain
Bulgaria	Johnston Atoll	St. Helena
Canada	Kenya	Tajikistan
Colombia	Kosovo	Turkey
Cuba	Kuwait	Egypt
Curacao	Kwajalein Atoll	United Arab Em.
Denmark	Kyrgyzstan	United Kingdom
Diego Garcia	Korea, South	United States
Ecuador	Kosovo	Uzbekistan
Egypt	Kuwait	Venezuela
France	Kwajalein Atoll	Virgin Islands
Germany	Kyrgyzstan	Wake Island

America the Beautiful

In 1973, Gordon Sinclair, a distinguished Canadian Journalist, made a radio broadcast filing a differing view of America in the aftermath of America's failure in Vietnam. Here are bits and pieces of his listing of ways and times that America had given aid (edited for brevity):

I read of floods on the Yellow River and the Yangtse. Who rushed in with men and money to help?

They have helped control floods on the Nile, the Amazon, the Ganges and the Niger.

Germany, Japan, and to a lesser extent Britain and Italy, were lifted out of the debris of war by the Americans who poured in billions of dollars and forgave other billions in debts. When the franc was in danger of collapsing in 1956, it was the Americans who propped it up...

When distant cities are hit by earthquakes, it is the United States that hurries into help... Managua Nicaragua is one of the most recent examples.

The Marshall Plan .. the Truman Policy .. all pumped billions upon billions of dollars into discouraged countries.

You talk about scandals and the Americans put theirs right in the store window for everyone to look at.

When the railways of France, Germany and India were breaking down through age, it was the Americans who rebuilt them.

I can name to you 5,000 times when the Americans raced to the help of other people in trouble.

Conservatives and Liberals Place the Blame on US

Pat Robertson agreed with Jerry Falwell on Robertson's 700 Club TV program on September 13, 2001 as Falwell told the causes of the 9/11 massacre:

> ".... God continues to lift the curtain and allow the enemies of America to give us probably what we deserve.... The ACLU's got to take a lot of blame for this.... the pagans, the abortionists, and the feminists, and the gays and the lesbians.... I point the finger in their face and say 'you helped this happen.' "

The Rev. Jeremiah Wright told his congregation on the Sunday after Sept. 11, 2001 that the United States had brought on al Qaeda's attacks because of its own terrorism.

> "We bombed Hiroshima, we bombed Nagasaki, and we nuked far more than the thousands in New York and the Pentagon, and we never batted an eye.... We have supported state terrorism against the Palestinians and black South Africans, and now we are indignant because the stuff we have done overseas is now brought right back to our own front yards.

> "America's chickens are coming home to roost,"

VI - Corruption

Offshore Banking Centers - hiding money

Offshore Banking Centers:	holdings
Vanuatu	$ 122,000,000
Aruba	$ 752,000,000
Macau SAR	$ 878,000,000
Lebanon	$ 5,119,000,000
Mauritius	$ 5,422,000,000
Barbados	$ 7,229,000,000
Gibraltar	$ 8,010,000,000
Isle of Man	$ 20,421,000,000
Bahrain	$ 32,887,000,000
Panama	$ 40,897,000,000
Netherlands Antilles	$ 48,701,000,000
West Indies UK	$ 55,814,000,000
Bermuda	$ 88,825,000,000
Guernsey	$ 94,205,000,000
Honq Kong SAR	$ 170,475,000,000
Bahamas	$ 195,451,000,000
Singapore	$ 257,282,000,000
Jersey	$ 285,398,000,000
Cayman Islands	$ 1,233,753,000,000
Total	$ 2,529,239,000,000

The Cayman Islands have 50,000 people and 70,000 corporations.

Offshore Banks – Big and Tiny Places

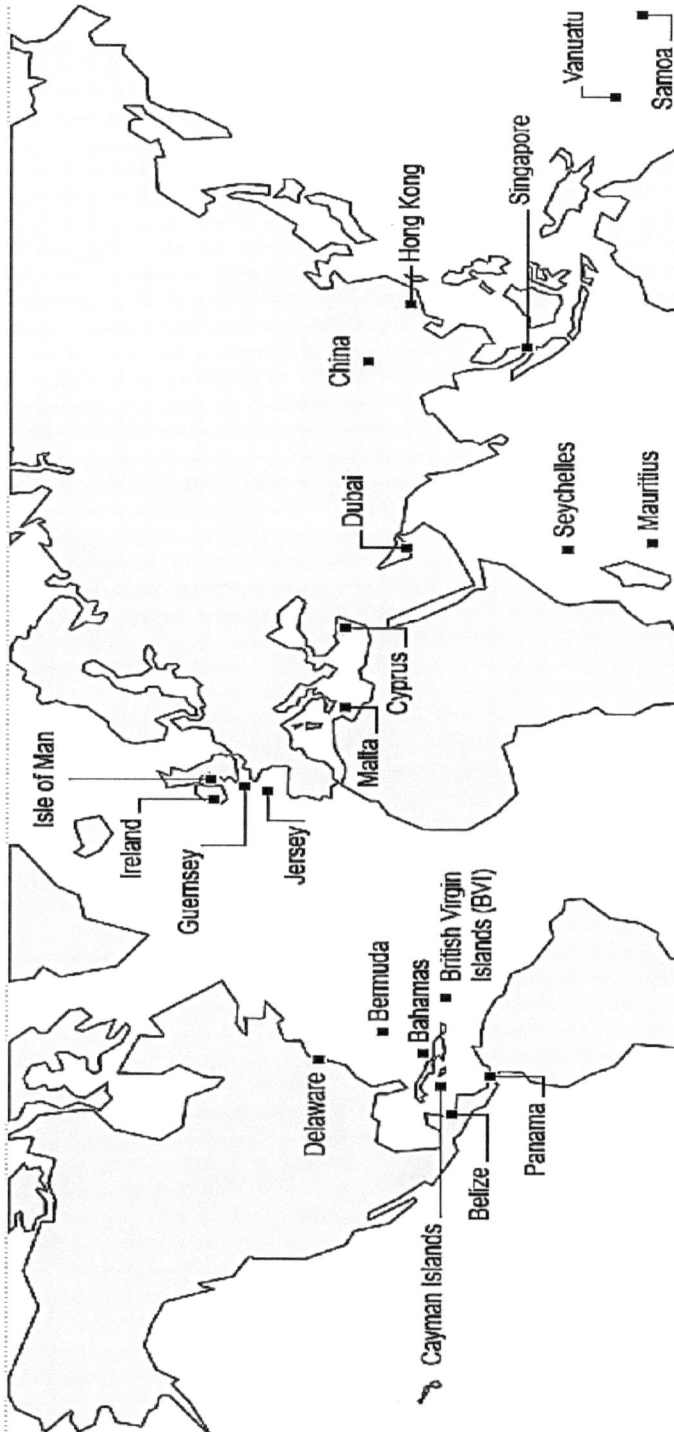

Michael Bloomberg – Former Mayor of New York City

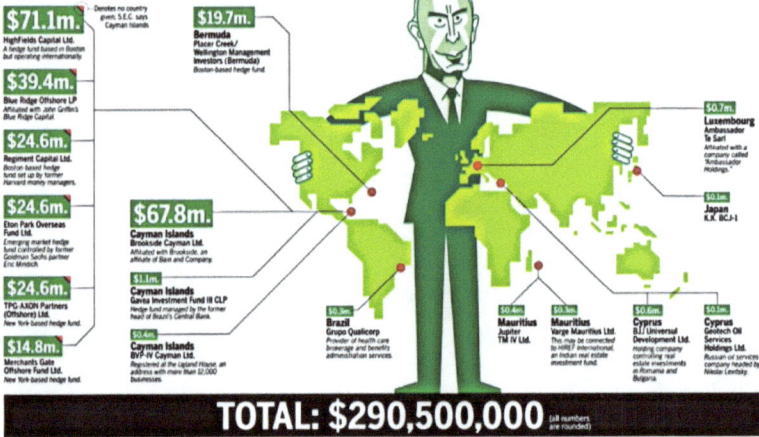

http://www.financialtransparency.org/2010/04/21/mayor-bloombergs-offshore-banking/

"The New York Observer published today an intriguing article on New York City Mayor Michael Bloomberg's $1.8 billion Bloomberg Family Foundation. The article states:

"By the end of 2008, the Bloomberg Family Foundation had transferred almost $300 million into various offshore destinations—some of them notorious tax-dodge hideouts. The Caymans and Cyprus. Bermuda and Brazil. Even Mauritius, a speck of an island in the Indian Ocean, off the coast of Madagascar. Other investments were spread around disparate locations, from Japan to Luxembourg to Romania."

Reasons for Banking Offshore:

Offshore companies are attractive for tax planning purposes. You can reduce your taxes or pay less income tax if your company is incorporated properly

Offshore formation can allow your company to become a tax-free company, provided it does not conduct its business in the jurisdiction in which it was incorporated

An offshore company is only charged UK tax on UK income. Foreign incomes such as foreign rental income, foreign trading income and foreign investment income can be avoided

An offshore company can be used to reduce capital gains tax

Offshore companies offer asset protection from lawsuits and risk management

Offshore companies and nominee services ensure confidentiality is maintained

Offshore formation & offshore companies are legal and affordable

There is no restriction on nationality for forming an offshore company

There are no restrictions on foreign owned corporations

There are no requirements to file annual Financial Statements

There are no exchange controls

General Meetings of Shareholders and Directors are not required

It is not required to disclose ownership of an offshore company

Financial Meltdown and Great Recession of 2008

How it happened

Repeal of the Glass-Steagall Act
   Republicans Senator Phil Gramm and Representatives Jim Leach and Thomas Bliey.

   Rep. John Dingell (Democrat of Michigan) argued that the bill would result in banks becoming "too big to   fail." and would necessarily result in a bailout by the Federal Government -- as it did.

Off balance--sheet accounting
   money-losing assets concealed

Lack of financial-derivative regulation
   Warren Buffet: "weapons of mass financial destruction"

High-leverage investing

Predatory, sub-prime, lending
   anyone could get a mortgage they couldn't pay

Federal preemption of state consumer protection laws
   using 1863 Nation Bank Act

Mortgages assigned to non-responsible parties
   made it impossible to resist foreclosure

Fannie and Freddie, FNMA and FHLMC, invest in sub-prime market defective mortgages
   On September 7, 2008, they are put under conservatorship and taxpayers pay

Mergers create banks too big to fail
   they are bailed out, ostensibly to prevent another Great Depression

Credit Rating firms give good ratings to high-risk securities
   draws pension funds into defective investments

The Rise of Too Big to Fail

Total assets of top three US banks as % of total commercial banking sector assets

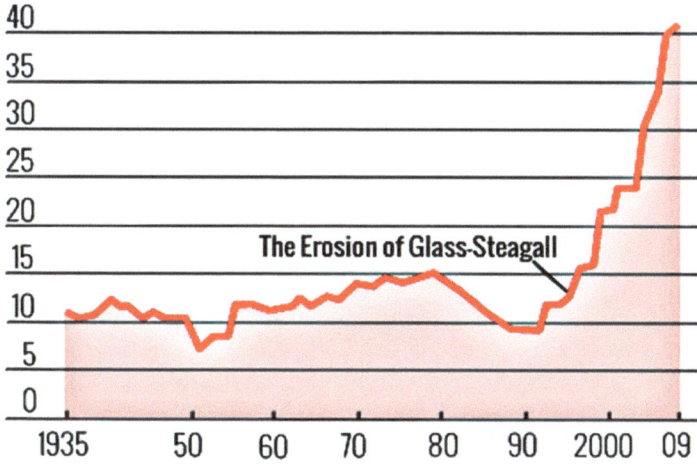

The Erosion of Glass-Steagall

40
35
30
25
20
15
10
5
0

1935   50   60   70   80   90   2000   09

Sources: Andrew Haldane, Thompson Reuters Datastream, Financial Times   TooBigHasFailed.org

TOO BIG TO FAIL

10 largest US banks, listed by assets (in billions)

1. JP MORGAN CHASE	2,389
2. BANK OF AMERICA	2,176
3. CITI	1,881
4. WELLS FARGO	1,436
5. GOLDMAN SACHS	959
6. MORGAN STANLEY	801
7. BANK OF NY MELLON	355
8. US BANK	355
9. HSBC N. AMERICA	305
10. CAPITAL ONE	300

source: TooBigHasFailed.org

Appendix 1 – Two Easy Ways to be Sneaky Wrong

1 – Ignore the Missing Facts – the Missing Subjunctive

"The state of the world has not improved,
therefore the effort has not been effective."

Call this "The Fallacy of The Missing Subjunctive." The cause is wrongly believed to be disproved in the absence of a missing fact:

what would have been in the absence of the effort?

This fallacy is common in claims of the supposed failure of government programs..

Examples:

1. Regarding the crime rate, the authors begin with statistics about the steep rise in the number of prisoners, then assert "Imprisonment has not solved the problem."

But what would the crime rate have been in the absence of the increased imprisonment? We cannot know. We can only speculate and theorize.

2. "The 'War Against Poverty' has not worked; there are more people on welfare than before."

Unknown is the number who would have been on welfare if there had been no "War Against Poverty." We cannot go back and try a world that has no war on poverty.

3. "The war against drugs has failed."

Unknown is the state of the drug problem if there had been no war.

The statement is invariably based on the subjunctive fallacy and loses its effectiveness for that reason.

5. "The U.S. intervention in Somalia was a failure."

Unknown is how many more would have starved if the U.S. had not intervened.

Your daily newspaper is filled with examples of this fallacy.

2 – Ignore the Stakes – Poker Logic in a Dog's World

The Two Criteria of Poker: Probability and Catastrophe

There's more than knowing the odds. There are TWO criteria for placing a bet.

   The first is the "odds". If the odds are good enough, you place a bet.

Some believe, very reasonably, that the odds of a great human planetary warming catastrophe are low, one-in-a- million. Choose your number.

   The second criteria is the "stake."

 What is at stake in the ecologic-catastrophism betting is the existence of human society as we now know it. If the catastrophe occurs, even in partial degree, the suffering of wars, migrations, disease, and starvation will exceed anything we can imagine.

Odds low, stake enormous. Who will play ?

Bjorn Lomborg advocates that we leave the table, and deal with the warming – perhaps less costly than stopping the warming.

Appendix 2 – The Fable of the Bees – Mandeville

The poem is too long to quote. Here is Wikipedia's summary:

The poem had appeared in 1705 and was intended as a commentary on England as Mandeville saw it. Keynes described the poem as setting forth "the appalling plight of a prosperous community in which all the citizens suddenly take it into their heads to abandon luxurious living, and the State to cut down armaments, in the interests of Saving". [Mandeville was much condemned in his day as advocating lawlessness.]

A Spacious Hive well stock'd with Bees,
That lived in Luxury and Ease;
And yet as fam'd for Laws and Arms,
As yielding large and early Swarms;
Was counted the great Nursery
Of Sciences and Industry.
No Bees had better Government,
More Fickleness, or less Content.
They were not Slaves to Tyranny,
Nor ruled by wild Democracy;
But Kings, that could not wrong, because
Their Power was circumscrib'd by Laws.

> The 'hive' is corrupt but prosperous, yet it grumbles about lack of virtue.
> A higher power decides to give them what they ask for: [Laws, Regulations,
> and Democracy – Honesty and no Fraud – a Liberal's dream]

But Jove, with Indignation moved,
At last in Anger swore, he'd rid
The bawling Hive of Fraud, and did.
The very Moment it departs,
And Honesty fills all their Hearts;

> This results in a rapid loss of prosperity,
> though the newly virtuous hive does not mind:

For many Thousand Bees were lost.
Hard'ned with Toils, and Exercise
They counted Ease it self a Vice;
Which so improved their Temperance;
That, to avoid Extravagance,
They flew into a hollow Tree,
Blest with Content and Honesty.

The MORAL.

Then leave Complaints: Fools only strive
To make a Great an honest Hive.
T' enjoy the World's Conveniencies,
Befamed in War, yet live in Ease
Without great Vices, is a vain
Eutopia seated in the Brain.
Fraud, Luxury, and Pride must live;
Whilst we the Benefits receive.
Hunger's a dreadful Plague, no doubt,
Yet who digests or thrives without?
Do we not owe the Growth of Wine
To the dry, crooked, shabby Vine?
Which, whilst its Shutes neglected stood,
Choak'd other Plants, and ran to Wood;
But blest us with its Noble Fruit;
As soon as it was tied, and cut:
So Vice is beneficial found,
When it's by Justice lopt, and bound;
Nay, where the People would be great,
As necessary to the State,
As Hunger is to make 'em eat.
Bare Vertue can't make Nations live
In Splendour; they, that would revive A Golden Age, must be as free,
For Acorns, as for Honesty.

In modern English: "Greed is good."

I heartily accept the motto' "That government is best which governs least".
Henry David Thoreau

The ultimate result of shielding men from the effects of folly is to fill the world
with fools.   Herbert Spencer

A wise and frugal government, which shall restrain men from injuring one
another, which shall leave them otherwise free to regulate their own pursuits of
industry and improvement....   This is the sum of good government.
Thomas Jefferson

If you understand the "Fable of the Bees"
          you understand the case for conservatism.

Appendix 3 – The Myth of Wealth Re-Distribution

The Myth: that unequal wealth distribution is normal – inherent in the inequality of persons – and not to tampered with. In fact wealth distribution inherently becomes unequal. One or a few will possess everything, as did the "Divine Right" Kings. Intervention is as pervasive as is the inequality itself.

Leviticus has Jubile being certainly a command for wealth re-distribution. The details are complicated and suited to the times. Note such phrases as: "The LORD commanded my lord to give the land for an inheritance **by lot** to the children of Israel." Lev. 36:1

Potlatch – a practice of native-American tribes of the northwest – is often cited as an example of wealth re-distribution. The practice of sharing was the wealth distribution mechanism of primitive tribes. One who was skilled in making arrow-heads did not accumulate a useless pile; he shared them.

Progressive taxation is as old as society itself. Charity and the welfare state are as old. Overthrow of oligarchs is as old as oligarchy.

Whenever and wherever humans gather together, whether as hunter-gatherer tribes or as the best 21st century democracies, distribution and re-distribution of the wealth is an inescapable, continuing process. I'll share my acorns if you pay your taxes for my welfare and social security.

The re-distribution into the hands of a select group, an oligarchy, poses a problem.

Thomas Piketty states in his 2013 best-selling book, Capital in the Twenty-First Century, that "the risk of a drift towards oligarchy is real and gives little reason for optimism about where the United States is headed."

Curious observation:

In principle, the top one percent of wealthiest Americans could pay off the federal debt (about $15 trillion) and remain wealthy by any measure. They have about $50 trillion and would then have a healthy $35 trillion.

Some References

Fable of the Bees
http://pedagogie.ac-toulouse.fr/philosophie/textes/
mandevillethefableofthebees.htm

Bismarck
http://en.wikipedia.org/wiki/Otto_von_Bismarck#Social_legislation

The_Beveridge_Report_Its_origins_and_outcomes
www.researchgate.net/publication/227976273_
Brian Abel-Smith
London School of Economics and Political Science, United Kingdom
International Social Security Review 12/1991; 45(1-2):5 - 16. DOI:
10.1111/j.1468-246X.1992.tb00900.x

Keynes page
http://www.forbes.com/2009/08/13/john-maynard-keynes-conservative-
opinions-columnists-bruce-bartlett.html

"Mao Zedong portrait" by Zhang Zhenshi (1914–1992). Mao Zedong portrait
attributed to Zhang Zhenshi and a committee of artists (see [1]). - Intermediate
source: http://www.flickr.com/photos/richardfisher/3451116326/. Licensed
under Creative Commons Attribution 2.0 via Wikimedia Commons -
http://commons.wikimedia.org/wiki/File:Mao_Zedong_portrait.jpg#mediaview
er/File:Mao_Zedong_portrait.jpg

Iolanthe, Gilbert and Sullivan, pictures
http://diamond.boisestate.edu/gas/iolanthe/mus_cov/covers.html
http://math.boisestate.edu/gas/iolanthe/bab/well.gif

Reagan: "Fascism was really the basis of the New Deal"
Interview: "I've Had a Bum Rap," Time, May 17, 1976
found in "The Fight for the Four Freedoms" Harvey J. Kaye ch.10, note.89

MAPS
http://www.yourchildlearns.com/geography.htm
http://web.mit.edu/newsoffice/2011/chicago-public-housing-0303.html

Communist Party rally in N.Y. City

the PWA
http://www.gwu.edu/~erpapers/teachinger/glossary/pwa.cfm

rural electrification
http://www.livinghistoryfarm.org/farminginthe40s/life_26.html

http://billmoyers.com/content/deja-vu-all-over-a-look-back-at-some-of-the-tira
des-against-social-security-and-medicare/2/

San Bruno fire – gas-line infrastructure failure
Source: Wikipedia Commons
http://commons.wikimedia.org/wiki/File:SanBrunoFireNight.jpg

the Corvair – wikipedia

Alternative opinion regarding global warming:
http://en.wikipedia.org/wiki/Bjørn_Lomborg

Great Depression
blogs.baruch.cuny.edu/his1005spring2011/tag/the-great-depression

Four Freedoms
Ron Paul's different understanding of Roosevelt's speech:
http://libertydefined.org/issue/20

East Germany
Feiwel Kupferberg. The Rise and Fall of the German Democratic Republic.
New Brunswick and London: Transaction Publishers, 2002. xi + 228 pp. $35.95
(cloth), ISBN 978-0-7658-0119-7.
Reviewed by Johanna Granville (Hoover Institution, Stanford University)
Published on H-German (April, 2003)
http://www.h-net.org/reviews/showrev.php?id=7461

Space Shuttle jobs
http://www.cnbc.com/id/43469916

Financial meltdown of 2008
collected from www.wallstreetwatch.org March 2008

Offshore banking, excerpt from:
https://www.cgincorporations.com/offshore-company-formation.aspx

Michael Bloomberg:
http://www.financialtransparency.org/2010/04/21/mayor-bloombergs-offshore-
banking/

Poverty
http://www.census.gov/newsroom/press-releases/2014/cb14-169.html

StanfordPovertyReport-2014.pdf see Wolff, E.N. Book coming

The Poverty and Inequality Report
The Stanford Center on Poverty and Inequality

Teddy Roosevelt
http://www.whitehouse.gov/blog/2011/12/06/archives-president-teddy-
roosevelts-new-nationalism-speech August 31, 1920 Osawatomie, Kansas

The Great Debate: Edmund Burke and Thomas Paine and the Birth of Right
and Left
by Yuval Levin   (a scholarly work)

LibCons-2-004.wpd